ENTERING THE DARKNESS

Christianity and its Modern Substitutes

Edward Norman

First published in Great Britain 1991
SPCK
Holy Trinity Church
Marylebone Road
London NW1 4DU

British Library Cataloguing in Publication Data

Norman, E. R. (Edward Robert)
Entering the darkness : Christianity and its modern substitutes.
1. Christianity. Doctrines
I. Title
230

ISBN 0-281-04537-2

Typeset by Pioneer Associates, Perthshire
Printed in Great Britain by
Dotesios Ltd, Trowbridge, Wiltshire

Contents

Preface

'So you will be laying up a good treasure for yourself against the day of necessity. For charity delivers from death and keeps you from entering the darkness.'
BOOK OF TOBIT, 4.9–11

The short essays which follow were originally addressed to the students of Christ Church College in Canterbury, to whom I am Chaplain, and were written periodically throughout each term in order to provoke thought and discussion on some Christian issues. The unifying theme of this collection – the difficulties our contemporaries experience in recognizing the necessity for formal religious belief – is expressed in both theoretical and practical sequences of contention and argument. As I read through them now, I see that some themes recur; the repetitions, however, are intended to illuminate particular difficulties from different perspectives. There may be, perhaps, some internal contradictions in the writing: what is offered here is not a comprehensive explanation but a series of passing observations. These are also, very plainly, observations of the European and North American world; it is always as well to bear in mind, however, that the decisive Christian developments of the future will occur in other parts of the world. Each essay is meant to be self-contained. In this I venture to be guided by Aldous Huxley's wise advice about the sort of book a traveller might find satisfactory: 'It should be a work of such a kind that one can open it anywhere and be sure of finding something interesting, complete in itself and susceptible of being read in a short time.'

Christ Church is a vocational College. We are largely, though by no means entirely, concerned with the training of primary school teachers and nurses, and our students achieve impressive skills and insights into the practical operations of their future service. But what, I confess, surprised me when I first joined the College was the extent of their appreciation of theoretical issues, and it is with this in mind that these essays are uncompromisingly intended to evoke reflective consideration. The generous response of the students suggested that others may find them a useful starting-point for their enquiries into what I believe it is no exaggeration to call the spiritual destitution of the times. The essays are offered with no claims to truth or even to a balanced perspective; it is hoped, nevertheless, that some will find them helpful in their attempts at spiritual formation.

Edward Norman
February 1991

1
The Quest for Meaning

Consider the realities of life. A small boat is winched from the sea, and as it crosses the foreshore some thousands of tiny creatures of the beach, each one of them a miracle of creation, are crushed beneath its weight. An insane child, incapable of communicating intelligibly with the surrounding world, is prepared for a lifetime of separation from normal human exchange. An aircraft falls from the sky and a couple of hundred travellers are scattered upon the landscape. Unseen and unknown within the blood-stream, a minute shape of astonishing and delicate beauty replicates and expires: a virus begins the transformation of its human host from vibrant life to horrifying death. Thus the great meaninglessness of existence, and of ourselves who are capable of detached observation of its course. Yet human society is not given to accepting a world of experience without meaning. It is, in fact, preoccupied with explanation – increasingly so, as the intellectual culture of the times, impatient of the account of things produced within traditional societies, presses ever more urgently for analyses which support the dignity of human life.

The less men and women have come to believe in the Divine, the more have they sought divinity in humanity: the new pursuit of meaning locates it in a materialist understanding of human phenomena. But whether men and women take a materialist view, or a view in which mankind has transcendent qualities, the demand for exact explanation remains the leading characteristic of humanity's present concern with establishing itself as the pivot of the creation. There are echoes here of traditional religious thought, which has usually seen mankind as the highest reference of the living world. Humanity, in this vision, was raised above the other creatures to share with God in the progressive development of the earth; and life itself is properly directed towards an exploration of the world of our senses, expressed in cerebral categories. The pursuit of meaning is thus an essential aspect of what marks men off from the rest of the created order. Is not the gift of reason the proof that humanity was intended to be taken up with the explanation of things?

The entire fabric of social advance is founded upon the supposition that somehow or other human life expresses a knowable purpose. In that sense the world can never be truly secularized, for the sacral values of society in all its forms and developments are testimony to the permanent existence of a universal belief that the ideas and artefacts of human enterprise are worthwhile – and, indeed, are thought to possess independent value. Though belief in a personal God or in a supernatural directive is diminishing in advanced societies, the succeeding world-picture is being filled with icons. Men have not dethroned God in order to establish a godless republic; they have, on the contrary, reared up new monarchies whose sacred persons, in the vestures of the sciences, make as absolute demands as God ever did. The new laws are not delivered as tablets upon a mountain; they are enshrined in the learned volumes of contemporary academia. The world is covered with meaning and explanation as never before – and none of it truly satisfying to the restless minds of the enquirers because none of it quite amounts to a total explanation of things.

The provision of universal education, and the impulsion which insists that reality may be recognized only in what can be measured, screened, and interpreted, is putting together a new world of exclusive explanation which will, perhaps, eventually issue in a terrifying tyranny of the mind. It will be a tyranny, of course, which will seem benign – for it will be founded upon intellectual discoveries – and it will enslave a people only too willing to subject themselves to systems of ideas. Human society is no longer a nexus of higher obligations, some of them hidden and mysterious, known through cultic agencies, whose truths are vouchsafed by initiations of eternal significance. It is now held together by acknowledged material self-interest, and its higher aspirations relate not to the beckoning of eternity but to a parade of human values and an incessant regard for human material welfare. Its temples are the places where ideas are processed into systems of meaning: the laboratory, the library and the computer-room witness the holy transports of the godless world.

What, then of the meaninglessness of the silent carnage upon the seashore or the value-illiteracy of the natural or human disaster? Modern people like to suppose that the world of today, with its bristling scientific knowledge of causes, is the first to encounter genuine agnosticism. They experience the most delicious thrill; for despite the systems of meaning there occasionally lurks a secular blasphemy: what if all the measurements and the data exhaust reality, what it there is nothing beneath the surface of things at all? The possibility is as shocking to the modern mind as it ever was to the religious. A great deal of contemporary agnosticism is actually a pretence; its exponents are really exceedingly alarmed by the option that nothing means anything. Yet, for all the modernity of the present guise in which the suspicion may present itself, that is precisely what so many men of wisdom contemplated in the former world. It was then known as 'the dark night of the soul'. The Saviour, before the resurrection, passed into the shadowy realms of the dead, and the saints and mystics of the Church, as a prelude to their advance into spirituality, frequently experienced some sense of the great meaninglessness of everything.

The men and women of today, again, like to suppose that lapse from belief in supernatural divinity is a modern phenomenon based upon intellectual enlightenment. But lapses of religious faith were, as far as it is possible to tell from the necessarily imprecise available data, quite common in traditional society – even in those spasms of time when people believed in the immediacy of hell and the proximity of the unearthly agents of divine retribution. The world of the senses had then seemed meaningless, attempts at truth vain, the sacralizing of life a pathetic evocation of the actual emptiness of humanity. Yet at the same time it was always possible to imagine a God who was personal and who had reflected something of the integrity of personality in his creation. How easily the second intimation may appear as a mocking accompaniment of the human desire to dignify the wretchedness of existence. How easily, also, the first notion may wrongly prompt men to conclude that the general meaninglessness of the world of our understanding excludes faith in a directive divinity, who yet withholds from his creatures a satisfactory explanation of material and human phenomena.

The difficulty now is that modern men and women represent religion, along with the rest of cultural evidences, as a system of ideas. Contemporary society desires packaged meaning in all things, and it demands that religion is no exception – a disposition made even more credible by the past willingness of theologians to package up their wares at the slightest invitation. Now, more than ever, religion – which otherwise lies dismembered and dispersed at the margin of human priorities, at least in developed societies - achieves respect only when it is represented as a system of meaning. That is not, however, how religion was once regarded. Traditionally it was the handmaid of mystery, an entry into an unknowable world. It offered initiation into the society of eternity, and it did not explain eternal mysteries. Jesus did not come into this world of terminal cancers and of crushed life in order to teach an intellectual method or a system of ideas which would unwrap the meaning of the universe. He did not offer hypotheses or certainties about the nature of the cosmic processes. He did not even praise the world of learning of his day (whose authority, in fact, in the Temple of Jerusalem, and among the official teachers of the synagogue at Nazareth, he appears to have rejected). For the wisdom of man is not estimable to God, and the Jesus who walked upon the earth did not offer meaning: the purpose of human life was never explained. Jesus gave redemption, not intellectual enlightenment; he spoke, not of men and women's quest for meaning, but of their sin. The spiritual culture he drew before them related to a landscape of duties, which they inhabited who were to be made fit for membership of an unearthly Kingdom, whose very foundations were laid upon the earth of existing imperfect human understanding.

The human dilemma is a simple one: it is not that the creation as put together by God is without purpose, but that men cannot know what that purpose is with the precision that intellectual culture demands. Enduring an interim meaninglessness which extends between present experience and the life of eternity, does not come readily to those who are successfully probing the nature of material reality. In the version of reality conveyed by Jesus the eternity of truth was opened to such as little children, and the screen which separates mankind from the celestial order was made up, not of false ideas or the lack of an appropriate intellectual apparatus, but of human sin.

The persistent tendency, by churchmen themselves, to represent their religious beliefs as an intellectual system - just like the other systems but somehow imparting higher and warmer values - usually involves imposing an alien grid of reason and meaning upon spiritual insights whose vitality gets extinguished in the process. Faith is indeed interpreted by reason, and religious culture will vanish from the earth, or be corrupted into something dark, if it is not rendered within intellectual categories which the world can recognize and value. But faith and reason are separate things nonetheless. Reason is the messenger of faith: what is being rendered communicable is objective and autonomous, it is independent of the means of communication. The systems of meaning which men and women in modern society find indispensable for interpretation of reality are anyway partial. They were not fashioned for the purpose of interpreting intangible and immeasurable phenomena – and a good thing too, since there is no true way of interpreting such things, except within the quite different disciplines of spirituality. Systems of meaning also shift and change, for the intellectual climate of the world is forever unstable. Truths about the dependent nature of human life, however, and the hollowness of human expectations, will last as long as there are men and women on the planet. Authentic religion points to the limited capability of man's understanding, and it will always show up the fearful manner in which the things which men create, including ideas, confine them. Real spirituality pulls away the accretions of human explanation to arrive again at the emptiness of the human soul in its relationship to its creator. Then they hear the still small voice. The divine nothingness within; it is an extraordinary contrast with the contemporary world's veneration of the depths of individual self-consciousness. 'Look at the surface of my paintings and my films, and there I am', Andy Warhol said. 'There's nothing behind it.' It is vanity that promotes the assumption that our interior beings are full of meaning, and that the transience of our lives may be compensated by the fixatives of intellectual culture.

2
Looking towards Heaven

The heavenly city envisaged by Christian believers of the past was, from the perspectives of today, strangely solid and realistic. There was an actual location, beyond the skies, and travellers from the world, in the deathless existence which succeeds death, reached it with every anticipation of joining the familiar society of the saints to whom they had addressed their aspirations in life. Because it was the New Jerusalem, and because the early Christians supposed, along with their contemporaries in the Roman world that the urban life was superior to the rural, eternity was perceived as a walled citadel, with gates and ramparts, and with fanciful dwellings for the blessed. It was, in another exposure, a perfect monarchy: an idealized emperor and his court, the Byzantine world – itself believed to be an icon of the descended heavenly order – in its most complete form; or a feudal ruler, surrounded by his vassals, raised up to judge the transactions and obligations of mankind for all eternity; or perhaps a sovereign of the Baroque age, his supreme authority radiating from a throne set upon the clouds, as in a triumphalist *trompe l'oeil* ceiling by Tiepolo.

Though these images were like the familiar world, they were also unlike it. They related to the splendour that people who were relatively poor in the material circumstances of their lives were able to desire in almost concrete terms, but which was, in their actual lives, far beyond reach. The clergy had taught them precisely about eternity, and its details were conveyed in single depictions which everyone knew about and everyone agreed existed. Hell, similarly, was exactly located, and so were the conditions there, which, again, everyone could be certain about. Both heaven and hell were very real places in the minds of those who inhabited traditional societies. Caught forever in the vignettes of medieval glass, or carved upon the boss of a vault, the very clarity of these visions of eternal life have a folk charm and a simplicity which beckon the modern observer to wistful regret at lost certainties. And yet for those earlier believers heaven was a place for the few. Their sense of impending judgement, and the reality of God's wrath – both characteristics of religious belief which Christians of the present day have considerably diminished in importance – gave the prospect of the heavenly city all the more solidity because it was the reward of denying the material comforts available in this life. In the modern Western world material comforts are not denied, and the prevailing visions of eternity have no need of recreating them beyond death for those excluded from them now.

In the modern world the idea of eternal life has become part of the emotional furnishings of individual choice. It is no longer a city with universally accepted features, but has become a country of the imagination. The clergy do not teach an agreed version of heaven, and no one would anyway listen to them if they did. For each person now envisages eternity as the idealized setting of his own private longing for respite from anxiety, for serenity, for the attainment of personal significance. The result is often humanly moving, and may achieve lyricism and even a certain interior splendour. Despite the theologians' insistence that heaven is not a spatial location, that it is a state or condition of things which mature people will not conceive as an extension of existing and knowable realities, the probability is that most people still see it as a place. But instead of being a place which is at once recognizable, heaven now has as many characteristics as there are those who imagine it. The world to come is the mirror image of the social and moral diversity of the present society of plural values; there is a multiplicity of images that corresponds to the hotch-potch texture of human sentiment which emerges from the television and media presentation of life. With the lessening of the sense of divine judgement heaven has become democratized. Eternal life is no longer the exclusive abode of the religious; it is the last destination of all the travellers upon earth, and will be as varied as they are.

As a country of the imagination, eternity persists in suggesting ethereal qualities to some, and a heavenly reconstitution of material happiness to others. In life the ideal landscape through which people travel in the silent drama of private reflection doubtless corresponds to simple emotional need: the point is that it is manufactured within the psychic impulsions of the individual, its only objective points of reference are those provided by the nature of the world itself. Some anticipate a vague idyll of aesthetic saturation, others a painless resuscitation of earthly loves, and some others an unfolding explanation of all the intellectual imponderables which in life had irritated the mind and teased the human pursuit of ultimate meaning. As a dying man, in his imagination, may rise from his bed while others sleep and visit the familiar scenes of daily life to bid farewell to the world of his attachments, so the eternal life of the imagination has become the translation of deeply held human longings into a vacancy where anything can be located. The past sense that the heavenly order was uniformly knowable, illusory as that may actually have been, is now superseded by a pluralism of emotional responses whose stimulant is individual desire. The universal monarchy of the Kingdom, like the political arrangements of the earth, appears to have broken up, its magnificent wreckage a reminder of vanished certainties, and in its place men and women employ a popular sovereignty in their understanding of the nature of eternal life.

Yet at the same time they are aware that their intimations of a heavenly existence are mere speculations. It is another way in which their view of eternity differs from that of traditional society. Once the heavenly city was a fearful reality: now it is an artefact of sentiment, an aspiration of the mind. The modern reluctance to allow public display of the processes of death, and the attempts to sanitize the actual disposal of the dead – and particularly to see that it is not included in the socializing of children, who are, in consequence, reared in ignorance and horror of the one certain event of their future lives – have given even discussion of eternal life a funereal atmosphere. There is thus nothing to link the country of the imagination with the realities of the eventual journey to its borders; the result is an insubstantial quality which hangs about it, a sense that it is all, in the end, unreal. Patients who face the certainty of an approaching death are encouraged to have a positive attitude to what remains of life. As a therapy this doubtless makes sense, and is in other ways humane. But it may also undervalue the nobility which terminal patients derive from their anguish, as the real issues of the purposes of death are suddenly concentrated into a few months. So many who are dying today have actually transcended the human horizons prescribed by their medical advisers and have discovered, once again, authentic characteristics of eternity in the imaginative landscape of our unexpected and often scarcely recognized spirituality.

Now people who have separately arrived at their own versions of eternity, and who have given them the personal identity of territories of the imagination, are unlikely to look to a corporate entity like the Church for any further guidance about the nature of the celestial order. Their understanding of the Christian religion is made to correspond with their own version of eternity, and not the other way round. The result is both a highly individualized interpretation of religion and also a decline of any sense that religious truth needs to be authenticated within an institutionalized tradition. Such people – and they now seem to constitute the larger part of the Christian population, churchgoing and non-churchgoing alike – have no doctrine of the Church. Truth is, for them, a matter of articulating a set of interior emotional impulses; it has no objective qualities and certainly no sense that individual emotional needs require the discipline of an external religious authority. Truth is self-authenticating, and the tradition of the Church simply does not come into it, nor does the notion of 'the Church' as the consensus of believers expressed through time. In this arrangement of things 'the Church' becomes, for them, essentially an immediate society of people grouped together for emotional uplift and for the doing of good. It is, in kind, little removed from a tennis club, or, perhaps more appropriately, a charitable organization. It is hardly surprising that attendance at the local branch, the parish church, with its economically distributed membership and its elliptical age range, is unlikely to have enormous appeal. The contemporary emphasis within the Christian churches themselves on the idea of the Church as community has almost nothing to do with a doctrine of the Church, and is all about Christian believers becoming a social entity to express fellowship.

'Whoever shall lose his life for my sake and the gospel's, the same shall save it.' The words of Christ remind us that the preliminary to eternal life is a cultivated spirituality in this one. The truth is that the heavenly city cannot be envisaged at all. We have no point of reference by which it can be reasonably located, and no indications at all about its nature. Christ himself said that in heaven there was neither marriage nor giving in marriage, that the relationships of the world, in fact, had no counterpart. He was himself, in his risen form, as he appeared to the travellers on the road to Emmaus and to the disciples by the lakeshore of Galilee, not at once recognized: a sign, perhaps, that the life of eternity is different in nature from the experiences of the earth.

Those who are called to the heavenly city must prepare for a transformation that is very radical. Far from Stanley Spencer's delightful and yet somehow disturbing scenes of the dead rising from their graves to familiar friendships, and to a happy and sanctified resumption of their lives, resurrection is actually to the unknown. Both the detailed certainties of the traditional heavenly city, and the personalized visions of contemporary understandings of eternal life, must be discarded.

Humanity, like all the rest of the living world, is made from the dust of the planet and given a brief existence before returning to it. At death everything that had been assembled into life passes back to be recycled in other life forms, as the world forever witnesses to the permanent mutual absorption of living matter. Thought and higher aspirations all disappear when the life of the body is extinguished. What, then, survives? It is surely not the 'soul' in any conventional sense; for people speak of the soul as if it is a kind of spiritual entity, sent by God into a child at conception, and then escaping the body at death to return to its heavenly source. It is, however, much more helpful to envisage the soul without these Docetic associations. The soul, indeed, might be considered as a result of evidence of life, not as the initial spiritual programming of it. The soul, in this sense, is assembled by men and women themselves as, during life, they strive for spiritual understanding, and for that service of their brothers and sisters which is among the necessary consequences of its discovery. And it is discovered through revealed truth, through the tradition of Christ's teaching. In life, men and women transfer, as it were, the spirituality they assemble, under grace, to the heavenly city. As citizens, already, of the Kingdom of Christ, through following his truth, they send ahead, to that part of the Kingdom which is eternity, all that is to survive of them. That deposit, the 'soul', is the content of eternal life. When the body and its sensory apparatus expire, that is all that is left, and it is already in eternity. Hence the crucial importance of following the Christian way. It is not a sort of elevating extra dimension to existence: it is the very stuff of eternal life. Without it, and without the struggle of the individual believer to activate spiritual reality during worldly experience, there is nothing to remain. Death is, in material and cerebral terms, absolute. 'Whoever shall lose his life for my sake', therefore, is to be taken in the most literal sense: it is the spiritual growth that is lost to the person because it has been translated out of the world altogether to build up the vital texture of the life of eternity. No wonder the people of the world find true spirituality so incomprehensible. They see spiritual values as residing in the enrichment of the human personality. But the saints have experienced, on the contrary, an emptying of their beings. They have become strangers and pilgrims in the world.

3
The Cares of the World

The men and women of today expect a painless existence. When they do not receive one they are liable to slide rapidly into religious scepticism. 'How could a God allow such things to happen?' they ask when disruption occurs to their scheme of disaster-free entitlement. Their understanding of God is thus shown to be a person or presence whose created order was wholly directed at guaranteeing the repose of humanity; or, to put it more as the men and women of today might do, God's love for mankind should be such that no ills ever afflict and nothing apparently arbitrary ever falls upon anyone. Here is a universe set up explicitly to cater for men's needs. It now seems impossible to imagine a God who sends people into a world of earthquakes and disease, and who evidently tolerates all kinds of human cruelties and meaningless misfortunes. A number of travellers are killed when their aircraft falls out of the sky; in the isolation of a hospital ward a young child dies from an agonizing and seemingly pointless disease; an earthquake destroys a village or a town and there is huge wastage of life; a student commits suicide in lonely despair. In the perspectives of the modern world such things seem an indictment of traditional resignation: it is no longer acceptable to regard these events as God's will, as things to be suffered without satisfactory comprehension because somehow the divine scheme is nevertheless being properly laid out. Events like these, on the contrary, are now more likely to be taken as indications of the divine absence. They are the human icons of an empty universe.

Churchmen and theologians often experience an inadequacy in the face of disaster, and some express a frank agnosticism about the ultimate meaning of human misfortunes. They accept, that is to say, the modern world's assessment of what should be the acceptable morality of the divine, and are puzzled, as the world is, by the evident gap between the ideal and the actual. Their God is not one whose will is conveyed by the apparently arbitrary cruelties afflicted upon humanity. Some, understandably enough, then proceed to make virtue of necessity by showing how in fact mankind is called to take part with God in the progressive development of the world, using the materials of the creation to eliminate some areas of suffering. Thus in medical research and through the enhancement of a social culture of compassion the suffering caused by disease may be diminished. And, through a more enlightened deployment of human resources, social suffering may be curtailed.

For the effectiveness of these endeavours it is necessary to recognize that there are two sorts of disaster to human expectations of a painless existence. First, there are disasters which are, in effect, man-made. In this category belong the transport accidents, or warfare, or natural dislocations like a flood or a famine whose incidence is made much worse than might have been by the inadequacy or folly of human social organization. Secondly, there are disasters which are outside human control altogether. By these are meant the primary effects of natural catastrophe, as in an earthquake, or diseases like cancer or AIDS which destroy life without reason. There is a certain nobility in recognizing that men and women are called to develop their finest skills and resources, and often to sacrifice their own self-interest, in order to bring alleviation to the suffering produced by both those categories of affliction. But for all that, and despite the considerable advances that are possible, the central issue remains unresolved: a benign divinity appears to preside over a cruel world.

The creation, in fact, is to be taken exactly as it is – a mechanism that operates as God made it to do. Despite all the scientific orientations of modern culture there is still an almost universal persistence of the idea that God somehow works by magical forces, that his powers are disclosed through miraculous dispensations. When a piece of contemporary scientific research, for example, discovers the exact mechanics of how something works – how the immune system of the human body operates, let us say – there is a strong tendency to regard the result as having removed the phenomenon from the sphere of the divine and to have in consequence diminished the idea of God. It is as if God's operations can be accepted as authentically God's only when they are inexplicable. It is as if the world itself was once a divine mystery and is moving towards being, eventually, wholly explained, at least in material terms. That is, indeed, more or less the case, since men in their ignorance have from the beginning of thought attributed what they could not understand in immediate terms to the direct operation of divine forces. Once thunder was recognized as the voice of the gods, and the presence of the divinities was made known through other natural phenomena. Now that view of the world's operations has gone forever, and men understand the mechanics of at least those parts of the creation. What has happened? God has been revealed as one whose laws of creation may be studied and known. The Book of Genesis describes men as being like gods – capable, that is, of reason and reflection and of joining with God in a progressive development of the creation. That is why the scientific research of the present era is a holy enterprise: it is an entry into a knowledge of those very means by which God has made and sustains all phenomena. But men still expect the authentic works of God to be magical – to be, by definition, beyond men's comprehension, and certainly outside their capacity to manipulate.

This curious need of humanity to recognize only a God whose powers are always mysterious is not the core of the present problem, however. That exists in something more serious and more difficult to understand for those worried about the seeming incompatibility of a benign God and a cruel universe. For a world whose mechanical construction can be explained could at least be a world of predictable order, in which the sequences of human lives could be played out in some repose. But in reality the laws of the creation seem to operate unpredictably, or, more precisely, unpredictably in the sense that they do not produce effects which correspond to human demands for a painless existence. It is the arbitrariness of fate that nurtures contemporary religious scepticism. The earth trembles, the floods rise up, disease ravages: the material causes are now plain enough, but how do the consequences for human life square with a God who is involved with the individual lives of men and women?

It is a wrong question. Consider the nature of life. God has created a world of living things upon an unstable material basis. Most living things are not recognized by us as particularly worthy life-forms, for they are bacteria, or viruses, or the typical life-form of the world, the insect. The unstable basis of all this, the planet, is heading towards eventual catastrophe, for, as described in the ancient myths of the human race, and in the Bible, the world is destined for final destruction: it will be burned up by an explosion of the sun. In the interlude human life has a tenuous existence and its one claim to dignity is that, of all the living matter in the world, it alone is capable of reflection and reason. The human record, as well as the authority of the Bible, would seem to give justification to the claim. But there is no reason to suppose that men and women were at any stage given exemption from the normal laws of the creation. God made them for a real existence in the real world. They are put together as other living things are, and their lives are conditioned by the same circumstances. When the earth-plates move the human settlements they have built upon their peripheries are destroyed in the consequential shocks; when other living things, bacteria or viruses, find a conducive habitation within their bodies their functioning may be impaired. When God takes away their breath they die and return again to the material of the earth from which they were made. The creation is unitary. It is interdependent. Life exists by the absorption of life, in a permanent witness to the common nature of all things.

Raised out of this through a self-conscious knowledge of God's existence unavailable to the rest of creation, humanity is amazingly given the capacity to use the created order to further the divine scheme. What is the result? Most live reasonably blameless lives of considerable inconsequence, preoccupied with the cares of daily existence, and unresponsive to higher reflection. Some devote their time to the invention of pigments that will render meat products more attractive on a supermarket shelf. Others set domestic contentment as the horizon of their capacity for living. All claim exemption from their humanity, cultivating expectations of a painless sojourn in the world; for whom some dreadful illness or a horrific accident will seem a terrible injustice. It is, as ever, a problem of false expectations. Men and women make quite unwarranted claims to personal significance and to a life-span free of disaster, and then blame the very substance of things when the desires they have set up are unfulfilled. They say, 'Why should this happen to me?' This also, by implication, suggests that life should allocate to each person the same levels of contentment and affliction. There is no reason, however, why that should be so. Each of us is actually owed nothing by life. We are part of the film of living matter which covers the surface of the planet, and are already privileged enough in having the gift of reflective thought. That gift, given by God, allows us to contemplate our place in the creation and to consider the nature of the created order itself. If God had actually provided the painless life we evidently regard as our natural entitlement the exploration of reality would be brief indeed. Creatures who reflect suffer mental pain: it is annexed to our humanity. For it is adversity and trial, affliction and disaster – and the mental capacity to recognize these categories of reality, which separates mankind from the rest of the creation – which provide the context of all that is noble and worthwhile. A life without the incidence of painful experience would be a barren affair.

The great achievement of humanity has always been its heroic capacity to discover permanent spiritual and moral truths in circumstances of disorder and imperfection. Although part of the creation and inseparable from the operation of its laws, men and women have thoughts which transcend their immediate surroundings. Out of this situation comes the possibility of rising to challenges, of extending the frontiers of human experience by testing ourselves against the grain of things. It is all very far from the contemporary pursuit of security and painlessness. The parable of the sower was addressed to our situation. 'And these are they which are sown among thorns; such as hear the word. And the cares of the world, and the deceitfulness of riches, and the lust of other things entering in choke the word, and it becomes unfruitful.' So lives are thrown away, or diverted from their true destiny; and the occasions for wrong priorities seem set to increase still more in the circumstances of modern life.

4
The Pursuit of Happiness

Just as men and women were not promised, by Christ, an explanation of the meaning of life, so they were also not promised happiness, the second aspiration of contemporary humanity, and the goal which most people today mention if asked to say what they expect of their existence. Happiness, indeed, is now so commonly regarded as the natural entitlement of man that it will seem perverse to question it. The pursuit of happiness, in fact, described large parts of the agenda of classical paganism, and it re-entered Western Christian thought only through openings made by French materialism and English utilitarianism in the eighteenth century. It has few, if any, traditional Christian resonances. But in modern society churchmen unthinkingly declare their recognition of human happiness as an essential ingredient of the divine scheme for the welfare of mankind: God is love, and the release of men from pain while on the earth is thought of as one of the manifestations of that love in the world. Yet although God is love pain remains inseparably annexed to human life. Much anguish is today displayed by churchmen addressing themselves to this apparent contradiction: how can a God of love preside over a creation in which there is so much suffering? Once the pursuit of happiness is allowed to achieve priority in Christian attitudes to mankind such an unnecessary question inevitably presents itself.

Christ did not promise happiness, and his depictions of the divine love, evident in the images of the parables, suggest the sacrifices of self-interest and the surrender of personal contentment which men and women must make in order to achieve spiritual advance. There are, in his words, no exhortations to reconstruct a world that will be free of pain, and no schemes of social change intended to further that end. Implicit in almost everything he seems to have said is the hard affirmation that the afflictions of humanity are permanent. He did not even mention happiness as the goal of life. And since happiness, anyway, relates to a scale of human expectations which has no stable basis, and no calculable fixed references, there was no way he could have done so which would have been consistent with his other, and essential, sayings about the condition of men. They were called to repentance of sin, not to a sanitized hedonism. The world–picture of Jesus implies something that contemporary moral culture is quite unable to accept: that most of what induces human suffering – fearful disease, the ingratitude of children, the unfaithfulness of partners, unfulfilled ambition, the great sense of loss that falls upon individual lives – is incapable of solution by social or political means. Today's world, in contrast, locates human desire, the desire of welfare and contentment, at the centre of its programme. It seems amazingly insensitive to perceiving just how unrealistic that is. Attaching the unattainable to a people of expanding expectations, whose emphasis on their humanity, in place of discarded transcendence, seems paramount, feeds the very fears it endeavours to eliminate.

The cultural tradition used once to emphasize the value of suffering: its highest point was mankind's denial of worldly advantage in favour of the divine service. It was taking up the cross – whose shadow lay straight across the path that led to a universal calvary. Nobility was recognized in those who reached out to challenges, who faced up to the stark nature of life and who sacrificed their contentment or even their lives rather than see their beliefs extirpated from the world. In traditional society this usually took the form of allegiance to religion, religion as maintained within a structure of society and government, intended to rear through earthly forms the nearby realities of the unseen society of the celestial Kingdom. It was God who was the sovereign, and not the leviathan of welfare happiness.

A life dedicated to the pursuit of happiness is anyway very dehumanizing. It is a secularization of the primordial religious idea of redemption. It locates it in the earth and robs heaven of its prerogative of judgement in the affairs of men. For happiness, at least as projected by its enthusiasts, is attainable *now*: no celestial dimension is needed to define its horizons. There is, however, no earthly paradise. The facts of human nature obtrude at every juncture of life and bring desolation to those who yet fail to see that they had grasped a straw. Do men really regard happiness as a fit end for human existence? It is to give up everything in living which points to a realm of values beyond the material and the immediate; it is to identify humanity, as materialists have always insisted, as nothing but a superstructural excrescence of the material processes. Then there is a winter of the soul indeed: humanity a chance assemblage of conditioned attributes, perhaps only the vehicle of genes, a race whose accidental capacity of thought and reflection is mocked by its own impossible aspirations to significance beyond the mechanics of the visible nature of things. Artistic and aesthetic cultivations are rushed on to bridge the appalling chasm in the status of men. The pursuit of happiness, apparently so benign, has actually disclosed the cold reality of the godless world.

The truth is that men have no way of knowing for what purpose human life exists. The Bible does not explain it, and Jesus did not speak of it – presumably because he accepted prevailing Judaic notions about life, expressed within the language of covenants and a part of the Jewish national inheritance. That inheritance, even so, was controversial in Jesus' day: there were radical differences among contemporaneous religious teachers about the nature of God's sovereignty, about life after death, and numerous other aspects of Judaism which might have prompted Christ to unfold a cosmic explanation. He did not do so. The purpose of life, of all the divine mysteries, is the most mysterious. For God chose to reveal himself through living traditions of spiritual understanding, through the religious intimations of the different cultures of the world, and through Christ, in ways which illustrated his relationship to the societies of men, and which taught the manner of living which is most conducive to recognizing the divine presence in the creation. He did not disclose what it is all *for*.

By negative deduction men can be certain that a God who revealed himself as a person, rather than a natural force or energy, and as a being who loves the works of his hands, can scarcely have contrived an existence of undoubted suffering if the purpose of life was intended to be, as now so often asserted, happiness. Is it really to be supposed that men and women are sent into this world of nuclear weapons and of AIDS to expend themselves in a futile pursuit of happiness – of release from the very material processes which God has used to create the creation? It is all so unreal, and the goal of happiness becomes a melancholy reminder that the terms of life were set by God and not by men themselves. They are called to take part in creative development with God, to use the materials of the creation and to extend the frontiers of knowledge about the world itself and about the relationship of men to it. Assembled from the dust, humanity is rightly engaged in the exploration of the dust around them, which coats the planet and gives them for a time, mobility and consciousness. In even the humblest individual life this dramatic undertaking is heroic. Men and women are inventive in the process of enrichment, whatever their intelligence or situation. What the task is not likely to elicit, however, is happiness. It is divine discontent which makes the world go around. The maturity of humanity is to accept that God, for all his revelations and manifestations, of which the world itself is evidence, remains mysterious. Now mystery is one thing of which contemporary society, with its science-based culture, is impatient. It looks elsewhere for its explanation of things, certain, still, that everything has an available explanation. In such a frame of reference the goal of happiness, simultaneously envisaged, remains as far from realization as ever. And there it will forever stay.

Despite all the contemporary rhetoric about morality and ideals, and so forth, it is also clear that most people are more concerned about the material preservation of human life than they are about the terms upon which it persists. That too, is in some contrast with the ideological requisites of the past, when men and women regarded life as the agency of higher service, and when the structures of worldly society were made to represent, however imperfectly, what were envisaged as the enduring truths of eternity. The transience and frailty of human life, and human consciousness of it, then promoted considerable nobility of character. This was not, of course, true of everyone: the pursuit of comfort through accommodation with the world is always familiar. But it is the higher aspirations that matter, the examples offered by the directing spirits and by the spiritual climate. Then people are pointed towards eternal destinies and their altruism in relation to earthly conditions is pure; today people regard enterprises of human welfare as the highest end that can be imagined, and altruism is embedded in a culture of calculated hedonism.

Once society was directed towards the unpleasing facts of human nature and the need for individual redemption; today public life turns upon the state of the economy and the provision of material benefits. The interior life of men and women is now taken up with a consideration of their 'personal fulfilment', their 'rights', or their 'happiness', and a consequential check-list of entitlements without which there is perceived to be terrible injustice. Once public life had to do with the divine service mirrored in the needs of people who were yet in the world: inasmuch as they were served Christ himself was honoured. Society strained upwards, and the lives of ordinary people were made extraordinary through the ideal, however imperfectly realized, of service. The pursuit of eternity, it is true, was often debased by too precise a view of the eternal, and by wrong claims made on behalf of the worldly institutions which were thought to embody its essence. The dreadful thing about the modern pursuit of happiness, on the other hand, is that people become imprisoned in themselves, endlessly ransacking their own emotional needs in order to attain what in reality is unattainable.

Many are today unprepared to defend their beliefs at high human cost. This attitude, understandable enough in human terms, implies that the survival and comfort of men and women is more important than what they are being preserved to believe. They are treated, that is to say, like creatures who are incapable of higher critical values. As values are always controversial, and are therefore divisive, their propagation involves conflict. But modern society is a great appeaser: it elects to regard human welfare itself as 'higher' value, so that all others may be discarded, or put up for auction, when occasions of ideological conflict are imminent. Everyone seems to keep clear of controversy; to see that men of accommodation and compromise inherit the earth. The ideals of the future are thus sacrificed for the material convenience of the present – and this is presented as a great moral advance.

The concept of individual happiness is static. It relates to models of the human condition which, once instilled, do not greatly vary through life. Yet life is full of change, and in the progressive experience of humanity there is adaptation and discrimination. These changes are always uneven. Some parts of human sensibility are more easily opened to fresh insights than some others; deeper layers of men's consciousness are less accessible to change than the ones that are upon the surface. The entire complicated assemblage of attributes and characteristics, highly unstable and not especially attractive – which is called the human personality – constitutes a volume of frustrated genius. Unlike the rest of the living creation men and women are given to reflection about their lot. Most of the answers to their forthright questionings are not available. Numerous substitutes, in the form of myth and religion and cultic observance, were once contrived in order to satisfy the demand. But they do not, at least in their traditional guise, satisfy people today, and for good reason. The intellectual culture has interposed screens of interpretation which have filtered out the ancient markers of truth. Into the cold emptiness of the godless universe men bring, instead, emotional and hedonistic palliatives. Aesthetic consciousness and the pursuit of happiness: mankind, in the act of seeking personal significance, has set up a chilling dependence upon his own substitutes for spirituality. Like most versions of cultural servitude it is presented as liberation. Into the meaningless world of authentic spirituality mankind has intruded synthetic explanations and false virtues whose deceptive appeal to higher self-consciousness is actually yet another substitute for reality.

5
Satisfying Emotions

It is a comparatively recent misunderstanding to suppose that religion is addressed primarily to the emotions, and that the emotional satisfaction of the individual is the most reliable test for the value of religious truth. Romantic taste and sensibility in the eighteenth and nineteenth centuries had much to do with it, eliciting a lush sentiment of personal reflection in which ideal human tableaux set amidst glowing vistas, and the achievement of an interior scenographic peace, replaced adhesion to received doctrinal formulations as the basis for acceptance or rejection of religion. But Christianity is independent of those who are its material agents, its authority does not depend upon their emotional condition. The truth of Christ's teaching has objective reality, and is not known about through dependence upon sentiment but through learning and living a tradition inherited from others.

One of the reasons for the astonishing frailty of the faith of modern men and women is precisely because they make it relate directly to feelings rather than to teachings. The age is impatient of dogma, yet dogma is the substance of revealed truth. Men and women today display great ease in laying aside religious formulae for which their predecessors in former centuries were prepared to surrender their very lives. They see human needs as transcending what they regard as antiquated and unnecessary attachment to doctrine, and they see this in a fashion which elevates the satisfaction of interior human sentiment as the chief function of religious observance. Liturgy was once, as it still is in Orthodox churches, a timeless reference for exact truth; today it is regarded as theatre for human values, a link between aspirations for a better society and a vaguely understood divine authority for it. If attendance at a particular church fails to prompt emotional elevation or a sense of human warmth people today will try another one, and then another. There is no structured sense of religious continuity, or of the duty of subscription to doctrines because they are true in themselves. There is no acceptance of the authority of a tradition of believers, of the people of God as witnesses and transmitters of truths which are independent of their sensations. The markers of faith are no longer discerned within the ambiguity and emptiness of the real world, but are imagined to derive from a campaign for an improved one – of a world of human value, without horror, which is all beautiful music, charitable impulses, human and social relationships purged of suffering and burnished with equality.

Contemporary Christianity wants emotional uplift without reference to exact doctrinal content. It is as if the emotions are to be regarded as self-authenticating, and acquaintance with supernatural forces to be made directly, in the form of personal experience, rather than through learning the categories of centuries of spiritual discernment. The sad thing about existing society is that millions of men and women give up a religion whose teachings and traditions of spirituality they do not actually know, their ignorance often sustained by clergy who are themselves impatient of traditional religiosity and anxious to hurry their pastoral charges towards the more immediate goals of human welfare. The lapse from faith is thus made gentle. Veneration of human qualities easily replaces love of God, and a new demonology arises around the political or social perpetrators of whatever human enthusiasm is at the time frustrated. Men and women are emotionally satisfied by a lush worldly moralism derived from the menu of human need. Then their feast is brief and intense, until they are called away forever, with little enough preparation for the journey which lies before them.

Of all the modern substitutes for religion it is the aesthetic sense which is the most esteemed. In appreciation of music, literature, art and drama, secularized men and women encounter a satisfying world of emotional uplift. The extraordinary thing is that many who are also Christian believers are no less preoccupied with aesthetic accomplishments, discovering in them an equal degree of personal meaning. This they identify with religious sensation. It is an example – and there are many others – of modern Christianity sanctifying its own secular replacement. That is not to say, of course, that aesthetic sense does not in many ways inform mankind about the nature of life, or that the divine presence may not be illustrated through the employment of the arts. And aesthetics as a serious intellectual enquiry is enormously valuable in integrating diverse perceptions of truth. But it is important to be reminded of the relativity of aesthetic accomplishments; for they amount to contrivances, capable of illustrating and eliciting any kind of response to any kind of prevailing culture. Being transported by splendid music, for example, induces nobility of sentiment in both religious and non-religious individuals in the same degree, and the same kinds of music may uplift Nazi and Communist, liberal and traditionalist, in very comparable ways. Whatever values are to hand will be appreciated with emotional cladding if the appropriate manipulation is available. Like the distinctly unemotional operations of a computer, the consequences can derive only from the programme. Differences of cultural awareness, divergent responses to conditioning among the young, the result of educational socializing, and an immense range of accidental circumstances, all issue in different people displaying widely disparate responses to aesthetic stimuli. It is very relative.

Religious truth, in contrast, is founded on dogmatic propositions, and its claim is ultimate because it is established according to authorities which are external to the individual and his emotional promptings. The secularization of aesthetic sense has been disguised by continued Christian adhesion: it is Christians themselves who now so often speak of their religion as if it were a dimension of aesthetic consciousness. The problem has a very large projection, since the autonomy of aesthetic sense in the modern world has been accompanied by a wider secularization of the emotions themselves. Emotion has been emancipated from 'serious' purpose, and is now indulged for personal satisfaction. Each person, furthermore, feels entitled to a rich experience of emotional satisfaction as a species, almost, of human right. Emotional indulgence has become an end in itself, reinforcing the obsession which modern people have with themselves. Aesthetic sense no longer assists the liberation of humanity, to be free of personal needs and united with divine service. It imprisons people within their own personalities, persistently calling them to feed their emotional promptings with ever-increasing quantities of cultural stimuli. Aesthetic sense has become the paradoxical handmaid of contemporary materialism. Its devotees see it as a 'higher' plane of experience, as a release from single-dimensional existence. But in reality it fosters the very fears it is supposed to allay, for it locates reality in the emotional needs of the individual and replaces truth with sensation. Cicero advised men against the cultivation of sensuality, 'for if you have given yourself up to it you will find yourself unable to think of anything else'. The same may certainly be said of aesthetic sense: it absorbs men's understanding and ushers them into a company which is very much of the world.

A century and a half ago Newman predicted that what he called 'accomplishments' (music, art, and so forth) would be confused with religious experience and finally mistaken for it. In the event that has proved a sound prophecy – and it has indeed been an understatement – for the phenomenon has been secularized even beyond Newman's imaginings. Aesthetic experience has now displaced religion altogether as the daily occasion of acquaintance with what are thought of as 'higher' values for enormous numbers of educated people. For those with less educational achievement there is virtually nothing. Concerts and secular music are routinely performed in churches as testimony to the supposition of many churchmen themselves that aesthetic sensation and religiosity are the same thing.

It is also widely supposed that there is a correlation between appreciation of the arts (as a 'higher' pursuit of the mind) and better moral conduct. Children are indoctrinated into reverence for aesthetic appreciation or accomplishment in the belief that this will not only enrich their lives but that it will socialize them in a manner conducive to moral self-consciousness. Religion was once taught with the same expectation, and it is indeed a further indication of secularization – of the replacement of the role of the churches by surrogate ideals and agencies – that children now receive their first intimations of 'finer' values in the guise of musical and artistic conditioning.

True religion, however, does not have much to do with moral police or with social control. Christ delivered his message to sinners, and was accordingly criticized in his own day by the righteous establishment for consorting with sinners. His religion was not a system for making humanity better, or more morally pure; it was fashioned to vouchsafe salvation to those who were not worthy of it. Justification was by faith. As many hostile observers of Christianity have gone to some lengths to point out, over the centuries, religious faith does not actually remove its practitioners from the ordinary moral frailty of mankind. It is not a way of sanitizing the personality but a gift of redemption to men and women as they are. Aesthetic sense is certainly the same. 'High brow: low loins', as Aldous Huxley said. The melancholy human record indicates plainly that lovers of culture have no more and no less moral sense than lovers of football or television game-shows. In one dimension at least, then, aesthetic accomplishment, as a successor of religion, elicits little if any improvement in the dispositions of men and women. At the very best a heightened aesthetic sense will make for people with a wider range of intellectual experience within which to express, and perhaps to understand, values derived from elsewhere. At the same time it widens the range within which human wickedness can find expression.

Art was traditionally the servant of religion. Now it is in the service of individual emotional demand. Where the religion was superstitious or corrupt, it helped to propagate error; where emotional needs are selfish or uncontrolled, art assists the cultivation of spiritual destitution. It has no internal compass of its own which automatically steers mankind towards 'higher' and 'finer' enrichment. The contemporary cult of aesthetic sense is a fitting substitute for religion, for it is the acceptable face of materialism presented as if it was radiated by higher values. But, detached from a doctrine of transcendence, aesthetic accomplishment is just another way of interpreting human phenomena as reflections of the material processes. It may seduce us into supposing that we are receiving spiritual nourishment when we are not. Arthur Askey described, in his autobiography, how years of singing in his church choir as a boy persuaded him that he had a vocation for holy orders. With time, however, he had the wisdom to recognize that emotional uplift is one thing, and that religious service is another.

6
Mere Morality

The suggestion that morality and moral consciousness are themselves substitutes for religion in the modern world will seem an unsustainable paradox to most people. Church leaders of even the most distinguished *genre* are greatly given to speaking of 'moral' and 'spiritual' realities as interchangeable. It is as if the dream of the dusty nineteenth-century secular ethicists has become truth: as if the world has found a psychology of personal elevation founded upon a religionless moral code. Moral awareness has now become the essential criterion of acceptance in modern society; it is the goal of education and the test of all political virtue. Men and women in public life feel obliged to give off their opinions in the resonances of moral language, for nothing less will satisfy either their own sense of the appropriate or that of their potential supporters.

Charitable organizations represent the secularization of acts of human goodness, and are the vehicles which now transport the moralists to positions of escalating ethical ascendancy in societies that have lost any sense of inherent human depravity. People have discovered, instead, an open terrain of moral certainty. The charities have the same difficulty about political involvement that the churches have. Should they contend for structural changes in society which, through political action, might eliminate the sources of misery, rather than remain dependent on palliative action to relieve distress? In practice the political world meets them on the same ground, for modern politics are heavily moralized, and the relentless extension of the collectivist machinery of the state has occurred precisely because of the moral weight of the various agencies and propagandists who have demanded government action in the different areas of their social outrage. No established church in the traditional societies of the past ever exercised such a thrall over the people, in the details of their lives and in the conduct of their citizenship, as the collectivist sovereigns and their omnipresent guardians of the public conscience.

Because moral consciousness is a secular replacement of personal religiosity it was to be expected that it would fulfil some of the emotional needs once met by Christian belief. A sense of higher service, of personal significance, of cleansing the world of evil, of purity: all these can be satisfied at the secular shrine where acts of human goodness supersede the impulses which formerly elicited repentance. The darker side of human emotional needs are also catered for. Contemporary moral sense is richly supplied with dogmatic and unpitying certainties about good and evil, and those who are identified as their embodiments are to be praised or execrated accordingly. The new world of secularized moral sense is extremely censorious, and shows scant sympathy for those who fall short of its canons; and is especially uncomprehending of these whose relativized assessment of the human record allows little taste for 'commitment' to the various causes and campaigns of the righteous establishment. It is one of the disadvantages of an historical education, from this perspective, that the historical scholar has seen it all before, and his scepticism about human enthusiasm for solutions to the ills of mankind encounters few understanding responses in the company of the morally certain.

Morality is rooted in the natural life of mankind: it exists among all people and is, religiously speaking, one of God's dispensations to preserve order within the societies of reasoning creatures. To say that a person is moral is to affirm only that his behaviour is in accordance with a general structure of behaviour. Morality is neither good nor bad in itself, but expresses a grid of predictability. It is the reverse of arbitrariness in formalized human responses to social exchange. To be moral is to be regular in relationships. Morality is thus the provider of a reference of social order within which the human theatre is enacted; it allows space for the cultivation of other reflective values. It is the essential accompaniment of natural religion, and, like natural religion, it is both universal and elementary. Instead of being the final grand distillation of human experience, and the very finest artefact of the human spirit – as modern ethicists appear to imagine – morality is an early stage in human perception of social reality, a low-level accomplishment only just reared above the capabilities of the animal creation.

It is, for all that, a necessary layer in the formation of the religious life, since the rules which govern relationships in society constitute the culture within which religious experience is encountered and interpreted. Of itself, however, morality is a cold affair of constraints and exhortations: it was against the supposition that eighteenth-century Christianity had become a nexus of mere benevolence and moral teaching that the Evangelical Revival projected a renewed witness to the vitality of Revealed truth.

For Christianity belongs to Revelation. Its *modus operandi*, the spiritual senses, address whole dimensions of human failure which moral declamation scarcely acknowledges. Christianity is religion: it is reared above the realm of the natural and its priorities are attached precisely to things in human personality that the derivatives of the natural world cannot affect. In religion, morality is taken, if not for granted, at least as a condition which people can recognize as a beginning and not as a conclusion of personal aspiration to enlightenment. Revelation is the tutor of spirituality, whose insights deliver men and women from the conditioning of the natural order and offer them what morality cannot: salvation.

The Lord came into the world, so Christians believe, not only to confirm that the discoveries and self-awareness of the natural order, including morality, were sound, but that what was wrong with humanity far exceeded the capacity of human contrivances (including morals) to correct. Jesus confirmed the Jewish morality of his immediate context. He made a few adjustments ('It was said of old time, but I say to you . . .'), and his teaching tended to translate moral consciousness from the collective to the individual. But the morality of Judaism remained more or less intact. It expressed the formalized social needs of a folk-wandering, and so confirmed for all time the general truth that humanity should regard morality as the depiction of a people who are in transit. Its interpretation will in consequence be relative to changing circumstance. It is the morality of the eternal pilgrimage.

Spirituality, on the other hand, describes the spacial habitations of grace. This is not of the realm of the natural, for Revelation is known in the divine potential of men and women. Their inherent bias to evil, as the inheritance of those who, being less than the Creator, are excluded from perfection, and their frailty in even the relatively simple matter of moral conduct, are perpetually distancing humanity from the celestial illumination. The spiritual presence is perceived more in shadows cast across material reality by its hidden light than in direct glimpses of the everlasting source. Like the candidates for understanding in Plato's image of the cave, the spiritually conscious are those who recognize the reflected images of an unseen form. For most of what is wrong with us cannot be put right by moral self-consciousness or by moral conduct.

Religion is a dispensation for sinners, not the righteous; spirituality is the treasure of those who may be morally extremely imperfect, whom the world despises according to the conventional tests of the morally pure. Morality appears to guarantee men in their possession of calculable benefits, such as order and decency in human relationships; spirituality gives men the incalculable gift of forgiveness. The content of spirituality, though disclosed through material realities, derives from God directly – seen in the person of Christ and received through time in the vocabulary of religious experience, of which the first and greatest instalment is worship and meditative reflection. If the machinery of moral consciousness is right conduct, the dynamism of the spiritual life is provided by prayer. And the grace which comes in prayer is available to persons of every kind; no intellectual preconditions are attached to its reception and no moral purity. When Jesus was condemned by the righteous for resorting to the company of sinners he was truly recognized as the author of a world's revolution: henceforth the Kingdom was open for men and women as they are, and not as successful manipulators of the moral law.

Morality, in short, is about the unattainable society of right conduct – it is not actually attained because human expectations constantly change the rules of engagement with the world, and because people succumb to lower standards; and spirituality is about the attainable society of those whose sin is so indelible that no effort of human resource can eradicate its deadweight, and where grace alone elevates. Moralists are inflexible in their attitude to those who are thought to espouse wrong ideals or to practice wrong behaviour; the properly religious recognize the ambiguity of human motivation and the universality of sin, and are merciful in not allocating blame.

The world of Jesus, in these particulars, is very like our own. In his day the Pharisees practised moralism in a particularly exact manner because of the close proximity of law and ritual within the Judaism of the times. In our society the triumph of morality over spirituality is so decisive that even the leaders of Christian opinion acclaim moral excellence as the highest test of gospel truth. In this, as in so much else, the secularization of religion is very advanced. It also assists materialism, for contemporary understanding of morality, especially as sanctified by the Church, is all about 'justice' and welfare. Now these things, whatever their desirability for other reasons, have no relation to transcendence; and in locating men and women's aspirations in the requirements of human society they do not readily assist the anticipation of eternity. The Christian religion is recognized with greater clarity if its spiritual culture is seen as fleshed-out in the moral order rather than seen as derived from it. The divine as disclosed through nature was full of splendour and may still be understood in the serene images of the Lord Krishna or of the Buddha. The divine unfolded by revelation, however, brings men and women the gift of forgiveness. Similarly the divine imparted moral sense in the natural order; but the treasures of eternity, reserved for those whose simplicity allows them an insight into the depth of their human frailty, give salvation in the realm of spirituality. The first man to enter paradise in the new dispensation of Christ was the penitent thief who was crucified with him: morality had condemned him to death, but faith in Christ restored him to life.

Human society, which is wounded by sin, incapacitates itself again through the elevation of the moral over the spiritual. That the Church so frequently appears as an agent of this characteristically human wrong priority lends still further sadness. The world edges towards the darkness by explaining reality without reference to the illumination of revealed truth; and men and women, unaware of their own spiritual condition, seek consolation and certainty in the ancient security of moral righteousness.

7
Divine Judgement

'Maybe we get little because we expect little.' Thus the wisdom of the girl leading morning prayers in the College Chapel as she assessed the spiritual landscape. The men and women of the Western world have chosen to adhere to an understanding of religion – if they adhere to one at all – which is an extended version of their material pursuit of security and contentment. They can only accept as religious truth what seems to them to be comfortable and conducive to a painless safe-passage through experience. Religion is perceived to be the heaped-up accumulation of the agreeable; God is love, and therefore he is to be envisaged as the great guarantor of whatever in life makes for human satisfaction. In its sentimentalized representations contemporary Christianity has become an uncomplicated sanctifying of the pathetic human disposition to seek basic emotional companionship, and in its intellectualized manifestations it amounts to a variation of the common humanist preoccupation with the values of human moral consciousness. In both it is less than authentic religion, whose central characteristics have often been exceedingly unconducive to the tastes of men and women.

For religious truth is about the creation as it is, and not as the creatures have come to imagine it might have been. God's love does not have to, and very frequently does not, correspond with human demands for emotional significance or for material well-being. There was a fashion, some years ago, for theologians to speculate daringly about the decay of religious allegiance and the 'death of God' (the supposed adulthood of the human race, 'mankind come of age') as necessarily associated phenomena. The thoughts and cosmic experiences of men, that is to say, had outstripped the capacity of traditional religious understandings to contain their insights; the world itself had become explicable and would eventually be explained. Ironically enough, this interpretation of things entertained itself by ridiculing traditional believers as those whose immaturity required religion as a prop to life. But a real understanding of religious truth has never envisaged religion in any such function, primarily because religious truth was recognized as existing outside the claims of men and women to personal significance or earthly contentment.

The blunt fact about religion which the people of today exclude from their range of possible opinions is that to be true it does not have to be, and probably will not be, 'nice'. God was not made for the service of man, but men and women were made to serve God. At the start of religion is human obligation, or the narrowing of freedom to use time as we will. At its end is judgement. Religious truth sets out a cosmic scheme considerably at variance with the human pursuit of security and emotional satisfaction. Both the call of individuals by Jesus to abandon the familiar companionship of families and friends for his sake, and the liberal individualism of social culture in the Western world which has grown since the last century, join, as if from different poles, to emphasize the loneliness of men and women in matters of ultimate value.

In the religion of Judaism salvation was collective; it was comprehensible only in relation to the special calling of a whole people. Jesus proclaimed a salvation available to everyone, but each was called on his own to the threshold of a new society of the blessed. For all that, it took many centuries for the implications to receive conventional expression, and in traditional Christian society religious belief and social identity continued to be inseparable. People still received their religious orientation from the collective, and the heads of families and of states conceived it to be their duty to maintain this uniformity and to strive to construct and sustain social structures which encouraged and embodied it.

Now, at least in the Western world, that has nearly all gone, and men and women are today expected to choose religion for themselves. Naturally enough, they choose what is likeable and legitimizes familiar personal needs. Some of these needs are in fact rooted in permanent conditions of human nature, and may properly find an expression in religious truth; some, however, are the contrivances of human insecurity as the peoples of the earth rebel against their transience and attempt to make their present pursuit of worldly accommodations matters of everlasting importance. Having privatized religion the state no longer needs to control it, and it has therefore been removed from the immediate theatre of public activity and been made a 'human right'. What is no longer a decisive social phenomenon may be defined with increasing vagueness. What no longer conduces to social control can be relegated to the chances of individual selection. Christianity itself, reduced to an affair of human welfare by its own practitioners, uses the antique categories of a largely abandoned theology to assure the world that the world's own concern for material survival is actually an updated understanding of religious essentials. When religion and human desires are made to correspond, the earthly and the heavenly are in unequal competition. It is precisely because religious truth is unlike the world's priorities that the instruments of salvation are known about in a special vocabulary of grace, removed from human expectations; they need to be sought out, like a pearl of great price, and purchased at high personal cost.

No central element of Christianity so illustrates the conversion of religion from a way of obligation to a way of personal satisfaction than the teachings about judgement. Very much of what the Saviour said in his earthly life related to the accountability of *individuals* (not collective entities) for their beliefs and actions. The parables are thick with verbal depictions of judgement: of the sheep and the goats, of the wheat and the tares, of the labourers in the vineyard, and so forth. At the end of time the Lord of all things makes some kind of assessment of the endeavours of men; these evaluations, furthermore, are not academic, and in the Scriptures are related to reward and punishment. So has the Church maintained in its teachings until recent times, and if it avoids doing so today it is not because even the most detached of theological expositors have discovered an alternative scenario of the last things, but because modern men and women simply cannot stomach a view of human life which terminates in circumstances of decisive discrimination. Nothing so offends against liberal humanism: a God who appears to violate contemporary belief in the sanctity of human autonomy, who sifts human values, who rules that life has purposes that are outside human determination. Worse still, Christians have always emphasized the exclusivity of the way of salvation. Those only are saved who acknowledge and submit to the unique claims of Christ: 'He that is not with me is against me: and he that gathers not with me scatters.'

The sacral values of the modern world are filled, it is true, with internal contradictions. No one is supposed to discriminate about religious belief, personal life-styles, cultural preference, or sexual orientation. But discrimination against racists, anti-democrats, sexists, and so forth, is considered reasonable enough. Thus the God who is acceptable to modern values is one who ignores differences of belief about himself or about the ultimate purpose of life on earth, yet who requires precise and accurate subscription touching the world's social agenda. A God who judges at the end of time has become quite impossible, however. Most Christians today are Universalists. Their conception of God does not allow for the notion that any will be excluded from paradise. The value set on human life by the prevailing humanism is so great that religion itself has been reinterpreted as a grand tribute to the absolute significance of men and women. God is no longer a judge, but a dispenser of cures to human ills. Some ecclesiastical dignitaries of the present day are pretty imprecise when asked about the teaching of the Church on such fundamental doctrines as the Virgin Birth or the corporeal resurrection of Christ; when asked about the eternal punishment of sinners, however, their agnosticism is succeeded by a frank avowal of disbelief.

Modern Christians have manufactured a religion whose substance corresponds with conventional ideals of the pleasant and the good. Only that is believed which does not offend against the universal desire for a secure and painless existence, now and forever. Death, if it is envisaged at all – for death is too much out of human control to be a fit subject for frequent discussion – is regarded as a dislocation merely: both before and after its punctuation human life is very much the same. The pleasantries and human affections on this side of the divide will continue in a glitzy rendering on the other side. This, it need hardly be said, is somewhat removed from the traditional Christian concept of the Kingdom of heaven, whose existence in the world of present experience anticipates eternity, not because of any pleasant sensations it allows to men and women but because it involves them in self-denial, and, if they are at all disposed to authentic intimations of ultimate values, in a cathartic appraisal of the earthly relationships which are so esteemed in the society of the world.

What of the men and women whose version of religion envisages God's judgement, if the concept is envisaged at all, as leaving the whole of humanity in the territory of the blessed? To what new heights of sacrifice and understanding has modern society elevated these beneficiaries of eternity? What insights have inspired their new wisdom? The terrible truth is that for most people their time on earth is expended in arranging the trivial details of daily living; the horror of human life is the worthlessness of most of what we do. The lot of man is to labour: it is unavoidable that his passage through the world involves cares and preoccupations which press against the realization of spiritual serenity. Nor was life intended to be an ethereal contrivance of spiritual contemplation, to which only those are called who are capable of manipulating their supposedly finer senses.

Most men and women, however, are impervious to the existence of the unseen world of spiritual truth in *any* of its forms. Christian faith invites people to recognize the permanent habitations of those forms in the familiar circumstances of their lives, to identify the presence of the celestial forces as they illuminate the commonplace furnishings of a mundane frame of reference. Christ and the heavenly order descend to inhabit the poorest lives, and their iridescence defines the shape of existences which before had seemed untouched by noble purpose. The broken are made whole; the ugly are made beautiful. All this splendour presents itself to those who love God. Yet most do not respond to his calling, and inhabit only a twilight where the shadows of desire and personal significance, of security and contentment, are allowed to spread out upon the surface of a depthless existence.

Men and women are in fact alone in the presence of their creator, and everything else is an illusory solace. Human companionship, and relationships of real love, may sometimes impart qualities of the divine concern for the affairs of human life, and in that sense anticipate everlasting values. But men are called to judgement, and that is both lonely and individual. Jesus himself, in many of his sayings, seems to indicate that the numbers of those who will enter his Kingdom are substantially less than the sum total of human life. Unpalatable as this unquestionably is to the worth accorded human life in modern society, it is what the Church has always maintained. Those who usurp God's prerogative of judgement, and themselves judge their brothers and sisters, are fearfully in error; so are those who attempt to discriminate too precisely about the beliefs of others. At the end of the day, and of the world, however, Christ will reign in actual judgement. It is an assertion which is so at variance with the modern construction of religion as a benign sanctification of life that many simply do not want to believe it.

'The Sabbath was made for man, not man for the Sabbath.' It was a statement made in reference to the idolizing of ecclesiastical regulations and ritual observances which have largely passed away. But it has an importance still. The entire structure of religion reminds men of their obligation to obey God. Obedience inevitably involves loss of freedom and may also, though not necessarily, require responses which cause pain – in the sense that our desires have to be laid aside. Human life was, for all that, created in order to enjoy God, and few, even those whose version of religion emphasizes benign characteristics, actually achieve that.

It is the absence of a daily source of transcendence in the lives of men and women which is the most distressing feature of the contemporary secularization of the culture. It is the more wounding to see how men and women ape transcendence in their dependence upon emotional simulations: these feasts of the mind avoid the realism of religious truth. These stark reminders of the interior emptiness of human lives are observed with the relish which greets a spectre at a banquet. The world wants emotional satisfaction, and it has it in human love and aesthetic sensation. The world wants a painless existence, and it strives to change the social institutions which define the options available to individual lives. The world wants justice, and it supposes it may be to hand through political engineering. The world wants eternal life, and its version of religion becomes a strip-cartoon forever unfolding a sequence of frames, each one of which is a perfected copy of present reality. Jesus calls men and women to a world beyond wanting, where true joys are to be found. It is, though few see it, the present world, where authentic joy is not defined in terms of immediate satisfaction. Christianity is about the world as it is: men and women are summoned to a reality, and not to an evanescent habitation put together by themselves, in which their frantic aspirations to permanent significance are given structural existence. The truth of religion, let it be said again, does not derive from our needs. 'And the Lord God planted a garden eastward in Eden; and there he put the man whom he had formed.' God made the world and put men and women into it; he did not make humanity and then fashion a world to protect them from the reality of creation.

8
Faith in the Charities

The emphasis on social activism within contemporary Christianity does not show any signs of diminishing. There are no reasons why it should. It is in large measure a reflection of the moralistic preoccupations of the secularized intelligentsia, who, no longer willing to express their concern for the conduct of human society within the categories of religion, have established an alternative network of organizations for the relief of social ills. The collectivism of the modern state now dispenses universal succour as once the churches did. The prevailing moral culture of human rights ideology, however much it may fail to achieve a precise and agreed theoretical basis, fosters a widespread conviction that all people of goodwill can sink their differences in order to serve urgent human need. The heroes of the day are not, as once they were, missionaries stepping upon a distant shore, or champions of Christian truth pitted against the forces of unbelief, but those who organize famine relief in Africa, or who devise retraining schemes for the unemployed of the inner cities. And their labours are indeed admirable.

It is a feature of the moral rectitude of each age that it supposes itself the first to have taken up works of goodness on any effective scale, or for truly enlightened reasons. In our age the organizers of the works of human goodness are certainly convinced that their endeavours are superior to those of the religious agencies of the past, which were, as represented in many caricature models, fatally compromised by associating the propagation of the Bible with the giving of aid, by making charity an extension of evangelism. Modern works for humanity are undertaken for the sake of humanity itself. There is commonly also a polemical hidden agenda: particular social causes are espoused in a critical demonstration of hatred of social or political opponents whose preceding conduct is alleged to have created the evils concerned. Where good works are attempted, not in Christ's name but in the name of humanity, all kinds of very human motivation get mixed in. But for all that, this generation is greatly impressed by its own capacity for moral consciousness in social matters, and churchmen are among the first to accept their declarations of virtue at face value.

Increasingly marginalized in society through the progressive decline in formal religious allegiance, overtaken in ideological manipulation by the rise of mass popular education, fraught with internal divisions about the real meaning of their message in the circumstances of contemporary cultural change, and unable to find an effective way of speaking to society at a time when communications are undergoing a sophisticated revolution, the leaders of Christian opinion are only too willing to discover in social activism a role which society will esteem. God himself is now seen to will the same kinds of social priorities as the dispensers of secular wisdom; there is an agreed moral culture, linking religious and non-religious educated opinion, in which the claims of humanity achieve a sacred character.

Not to share in contemporary social enthusiasms is to be relegated, by the leading churchmen of the day, to the peripheral and outmoded 'piety of other-worldliness'; it is to appear indifferent to the world's moral sense, and to be set, along with Christians of the past, into the enclosure of execration reserved for those who cultivate interior spirituality and leave the socially disadvantaged to fester unattended in their various miseries. There is nothing particularly subtle about the propaganda of contemporary moralism, but it seems so self-evidently true that its advocates, especially within the churches, are intolerant of alternatives. And because Christians are called to love of neighbour, and because Christ's calling to individuals can only be effectively expressed by concern for the fate of others, there can be no quarrel with the ideal of human compassion – though there can be with the appropriate means by which it is organized. The churches have given very sympathetic backing to collectivist solutions for social problems: they have, that is to say, supported a high level of state power to use the force of law to compel certain types of social alleviation. That was the burden of the Church of England's report of 1985, *Faith in the City*, for example. The real issue, underlying the simple goodness of the intentions of advanced collectivism, is whether it is right to use the power of the state to enforce Christian beliefs – in this case, belief in social engineering. Clearly there are very wide considerations opening up here, and they may be taken as indicators that in the movement from intention to action the churches' contemporary commitment to social issues involves some unresolved – indeed unasked – theoretical questions.

The point in the present context, however, is that the churches' endorsement of enlightened social policy has not attracted any new following in society itself. That was not, of course, the purpose: social issues have been taken up for their own sake, because they seemed the right way of expressing Christian love of neighbour. But there has also been an accompanying rhetoric of social compassion, widely employed by church leaders, which has frankly suggested that Christian involvement with social issues is one of the ways in which Christianity can appear 'relevant' to existing society. Any such expectation has been largely unfulfilled. This is partly because of the general amalgam of complex reasons which explain why modern people do not resort to religious institutions, and partly because of another important development. The churches have defined a social role, but the public know there are agencies which are better at carrying it out than they are.

The contemporary rise of the great charitable organizations amounts to the establishment of a substitute church. For this they have a number of advantages. They are largely uncontroversial: no one has to worry about which particular style to adopt, for the charities' message of human need does not require a ceremonial or ritual structure. They can rely on being largely uncriticized – few are going to venture to question the doing of social good, where the recipients are the victims of disease or disaster, or social unfortunates whose plight afflicts the conscience.

Like the Church in traditional society, the charities hold out a terrifying eschatology. Unless urgent action is taken some fearful catastrophe will happen to the human race because of this or that revelation of impending dislocation. People seem to feel the need for eschatological terror. The ultimate visions of hell and judgement are now gone; in their place, however, are the secularized torments of a depleted ozone layer, or the warming of the earth. The charities are the harbingers of information about human disaster. They bring news of horrific suffering, and offer the chance for ordinary people to participate and to expiate through financial giving.

Like the salvation held out to believers in past societies where religion seemed decisive, the charities can offer actual relief of human suffering through the relatively painless offering of sums of money. They satisfy contemporary moralism: there is always some social group, or some economic system, or some structure of government, which can be blamed, if not for causing disaster, at least for impeding the successful implementation of whatever solution the organizers of the charities declare to be appropriate. For the charities are holy. They may periodically attract criticism because of some feature of their internal administration, just as reformers once sought to restore the purity of the Church; but their essential message is elevated beyond question, for it has to do with this sacred character of human need. The temples of the charities are the television screens. Only a few years ago media discussions about moral issues always had a token churchman on the panel; now he is gone, and his place is taken by an official of one of the charitable organizations. These people even have the power of influence which the churches once possessed. When their presentation of a particular social ill is pressed with insistence, it eventually achieves the agenda of government. The media presenters look to the propaganda of the charities, and not to the churches, for material about the moral state of mankind.

The rise of the charitable organizations may therefore be seen as providing direct replacements of the churches. They fulfil so many of the needs that religion once furnished, and they have the great advantage that they are listened to with respect. The funds at their disposal compare with those available to the churches in the expansive decades of the last century. Those who would once have satisfied an inner twinge of piety by supporting a religious work now make a donation to OXFAM instead. The vicarious element has an obvious appeal, since the obligations of human decency may be attended to from an armchair, while at the same time actual and important work of social relief is achieved. A religion of good works exactly corresponds to the inclinations of many in Western society – and especially the English, for whom the doctrines of Christianity were anyway always secondary to the practical works of religious bodies. There has been an impatience with a religion expressed in dogma and disclosed to the faithful through a clerical hierarchy. It has seemed, to many, wrong to put religious ideas before practical good done to others. Love of neighbour as a precedence over love of God has never seemed improper in the popular culture: where God is envisaged as a provider of satisfactory emotional reassurance, and a dealer in benign fortune, the two scarcely had to be separated.

Traditional anti-clericalism now persists only in the dusty prejudices of a few; once, however, it expressed a very real belief that the priesthood had converted true religion into a mysterious affair of abstruse doctrinal formulations, and had diverted the giving of alms from support for the distressed and needy into the wealth of a corrupted ecclesiastical institution. Anti-clericalism diminished as the Church lost its social influence: there was no need to oppose a body of men who had no opportunity to interfere in the normal conduct of life. The existing social priorities of the Church have finally buried it, for social activism matches the public understanding of what the Church should be doing – provided, of course, that it is non-partisan in a political sense, for the public, also, is unhappy about the mixture of politics and religion. No one wants to be told by the clergy how to behave politically. They like to think of the clergy as uncomplicated people with moral intentions, who do not insist on precise theological positions (while somehow remaining orthodox), who regard doctrine as subordinate to good works, and whose love of humanity equals their own. The churches of the present day are well provided with exemplars of their ideals.

But all this is still at the fringe. It remains a problem for the clergy that however much they emphasize the pastoral and social functions of religion the people to whom they believe themselves sent persist in indifference to the Church itself. The people like a clergy with a social conscience but do not regard the Church as a proper agency for effective social action. Where the Church enters the popular imagination at all it is as the visual accompaniment of the rites of passage, over which, anyway, the clergy in practice still operate something of a monopoly. Otherwise, to the everlasting frustration of the clergy themselves, and to the detached amusement of the littérateurs, the Church seems little more than a chance survivor of traditional society, whose decline is widely lamented but whose existence few care to assist. That the Church is the eternal society of those who, as the Saviour promised, have overcome the world, is not among the popular options. Perhaps there has been too close a scrutiny of the inheritors of eternal life as they sit upon their pews.

9
Church Teaching and Clergy Learning

The official teachers of Christianity not only have some difficulty in determining their social role in a society that evidently feels able to sustain itself without them; they also have a problem with the nature of their teaching itself. For once they were virtually the only educated men, and in each parish they provided a whole range of services for their illiterate flocks which made them indispensable for reasons that had nothing to do with religion at all. They were the source of news from the wider society, the men of wisdom whose reading allowed references almost unimagined by ordinary people, and the purveyors of what education was available to aspirant elements within the local population. It is probably no exaggeration to say that the clergy were responsible for the formation of minds – although it would probably also be easy to exaggerate the extent to which, in practice, many minds were actually formed through their efforts. Not all the clergy were efficient, or resided in their parishes, and a romantic view of traditional society, in which social exchanges and the pervasiveness of deference allowed a uniform transference of values, can be over-drawn. Nevertheless, until comparatively recent times, and until the expansion of urban populations finally outstripped the capacity of ecclesiastical resources, church influence was considerable, and in most places decisive, in the acquisition of knowledge and values by ordinary people.

It became clear, at the end of the eighteenth century and at the start of the nineteenth, that the population shifts attendant upon industrialization were creating large areas which were outside the traditional parochial ministrations of the Church. The leadership of the Church responded with a programme of new church building, and with the establishment of church schools. They received the support of government: there was widespread apprehension of a threat to social order should the enlarged population escape the social control of which religious values were regarded as an important part. The idealism of church extension, the mission to the urban masses – and the contemporaneous expansion of overseas missions inspired by the colonial exploits of the European powers – gave a buoyancy to Christian endeavour, and attracted the enthusiasm of the bourgeoisie, which issued in the great nineteenth-century boom in Christianity. It was actually a modest boom in numerical terms, at least in the home countries, and did not even keep pace with the expansion of the population; but the educated classes made Christianity the vehicle of moral seriousness, and the role of the clergy as teachers of religion received a renewed social endorsement.

At the same time, however, education itself was escaping from clerical control. The collectivism of the state began to move into educational provision when it became clear that the financial resources available to the churches were inadequate to meet the needs of the growing population. When denominational rivalries questioned the kind of Christian teaching that the state should sanction in its own schools, and led to political controversy, the teaching of the state schools became less and less susceptible to the influence of the clergy. Intellectual difficulties about the nature of religious belief, which modern intellectuals see as the most decisive reason, as they would, for the emancipation of education from clerical supervision, eventually had some influence. The result, in the twentieth century, has been a society which does not look to Christian organizations to provide mass education, although in many countries the traditional role of the churches in conducting schools of their own, with or without government financial assistance, continues.

The result also is that the clergy, so far from being the only educated people in most localities, are now, from the perspective of educational resource, indistinguishable from the literate society around them. Does that make them more liable to absorb the secularized values of the largely secularized intelligentsia? Perhaps so, though many other considerations, including a loss of confidence in the unique nature of religious phenomena, are probably mainly responsible. The chief difficulty for the clergy is that they are, intellectually, no more qualified than their flocks at the discernment of information and the formation of opinion. They are operating in a culture where it can no longer be assumed that the local representative of the Church is a person of any significant intellectual ability. Relative to the educational attainment of their flocks, furthermore, it is not just that a parity has been reached but that the clergy are sinking. The intellectual capabilities of the clergy of the past can doubtless be exaggerated.

But there is no doubt about the diminished abilities of the clergy of today: the simple fact is that the finest minds, those who emerge at the highest levels of educational training, are not seeking ordination to the ministry of the Church.

In many Western Churches the decline in the intellectual quality of the clergy has been disguised by an increase in mature vocations. Those coming forward for ordination often have solid professional qualifications originally gained for entry into other work, which then becomes available to the Church. The increase in the ministry of women makes available a whole range of intellectual talent which, because of the modest part women have formerly taken in professional life, had before been largely unused. For all that, however, the fact is that the clergy of today are unquestionably less educationally gifted, in relation to those around them in comparable areas of professional life, than they have ever been. This is true for Europe and the United Kingdom, and it is beginning to be true for the United States, where a high level of religious affiliation, and a very professional clergy, have for so long maintained what has probably been the most educated Christian ministry the world has ever seen. At this point it is usual to add that the pastoral gifts of the clergy today, and their vocational sense, is such as easily to compensate for their lack of learning. So be it.

In what sense, however, can the people who aspire to religious information or direction, who need, in short, instruction in the faith, get this from a clergy who may be considerably less educationally accomplished than they are themselves? If it was a question of *spiritual* direction the question would hardly be apposite, for spiritual wisdom is independent of formal learning, and spiritual gifts were first delivered, in the Christian dispensation, to fishermen of Galilee. But the ministry of the Church is not, today, particularly characterized by spirituality. The emphasis on pastoral work and on social activism is not conceived within a religious culture of spiritual discernment but with social knowledge and social issues as the first frame of reference. Ordination candidates are liable to be more intimately acquainted with serial data about social deprivations than they are with the insights of the mystics and doctors of the Christian tradition. The people to whom they listen, in their earliest ministry, are more likely to speak of the hardships caused by the levels of government funding for the social services than they are of the ambiguities of interior suffering or the desolation of the soul. The clergy are concerned with precisely the same world of educational values as the people among whom they are sent. That sounds right – how better to speak to the people, than when the vocabulary of information is shared? – until it is realized that the people are probably very much better at the discussion of those values than the clergy are. Having produced an understanding of Christianity that fosters an engagement with the issues of the day, and recognizing human problems as residing in the circumstances of their lives rather than in the effects of their natures, the clergy have intellectual capacities that in no way enable them to transcend the conventional area of debate. Their voice is no different to that of anyone else. Their agenda is set by the world of social moralism: spiritual discernment is overlaid by moral judgement.

A couple of decades ago it was noticeable that many of the young clergy in training, and a number of those who had been in the ministry for many years, were undergoing crises of identity. They were really quite hard put to it to explain what their vocation meant because they could not satisfactorily define what religion itself meant. That degree of spiritual disorientation is now less frequently encountered. Doubtless the increase in vocations from the Evangelical wing of Protestantism has helped to blow it away. Evangelicals are usually pretty precise about their vocations, since the Bible has uncomplicated directives which they receive uncomplicatedly. Though there are fewer personal crises, however, Christianity itself, in the hands of the clergy, has become more and not less personalized. Each minister no longer appears to see himself as constrained to teach what the Church declares, but to construct an understanding of Christianity for himself. For some, this makes the faith something which is healthily compatible with the social moralism or the intellectual culture of the day. Even the Evangelicals, whose *penchant* for contemporary parables is well known, are rather given to using examples from public discussion which hint at an extensive acquaintance with the issues of public opinion. In view of the fact that the official teachings of the Church are sometimes difficult to discover, this tendency to individualize understanding of the faith may be understandable. Who is to say, for example, what is the doctrine of the Church itself taught by Anglicans, or whether the Methodists hold to the Double Procession of the

Holy Spirit? The difficulty raised by the clergy constructing their own interpretations of the faith, however, is practical as well as being a matter of authority. For their intellectual limitations are such that the resulting package of knowledge is as likely to irritate and confuse their hearers as it is to help or instruct them. Church members, and the public at large, want to know what the Church teaches – what centuries of accumulated piety distils, what generations of spiritual discernment can now bring forward. Instead, they are met by a myriad of different voices, each one of which seeks to give a religious gloss to the agenda of the age, expressed in the categories of contemporary informed discourse.

Some of the issues of public discussion about which a religious view is sought are, it is true, so novel that the necessary applications of theological insight may not have had time to mature, or they may have already engendered such controversy as to make an agreed theological response impossible. Questions like the mechanics of human fertilization may be of this sort. But the general picture is much more inclusive. It is of a clergy who give off their own opinions when asked to instruct in the teachings of the Church which employs them. The public discovers, in the process, that the clergy are often less qualified than they are themselves to hold opinions in the areas of debate at issue, and that what is offered as Christian teaching turns out to be a mere expression of individual preference. The result is, by any standards, profoundly unsatisfactory. It is a real problem for religion in contemporary society that there is no *corps* of religious officials consistently giving off an agreed statement of Christian teaching. Where else are the public to look? It is a sad coincidence that the clergy should resort to private opinion in order to render Christianity intellectually respectable at just that moment in the history of the Church when their own intellectual capabilities are in decline. The general liberal tone of Western society, furthermore, inhibits ecclesiastical authority, even in the Roman Catholic Church, from seeking to restore the role of religious authority. The result is a religion of private enterprise, in which it is not clear that those seeking orthodox instruction in the faith will know where to look.

10
Doctrine and Teaching

Reflections on the propriety of the clergy constructing individualized understandings of Christianity should not be taken to imply that Christian teaching has been fixed for all time, and requires no kind of adjustment or reinterpretation. Unhappily there is no agreement within the leadership of the Churches about either the extent of any necessary changes or the mechanism by which they may be achieved. The second is the more important: there will always be divisions of view, but a consensus of the faithful which is of sufficient velocity to carry adjustment forward should neither advance too rapidly, nor fall too far behind expectations. It is a situation which, from different poles, causes an enormous amount of external criticism as well, and deters many from allegiance to organized religion. Those whose inclinations are towards considerable reinterpretation of Christian truth, in order to render it more compatible, as they would see it, with contemporary intellectual culture and with the conditions of modern society, are impatient with the modesty of the efforts in their direction. Those conservatives and traditionalists who sense that change is in itself unnecessary, and whose suspicions of the leadership are fed by the impression that extensive adjustments are impending, are already slipping away from the Church in a steady demonstration of disillusionment. In all of the Churches, as it happens, there has actually been more talk than action, and real shifts in the interpretation of the faith have been comparatively slight – certainly less than the public, unnecessarily alarmed by the speculations of progressive academic theologians, have supposed. It has been in religious worship and symbolism that most changes have occurred, and these, while affecting the keenest sense of personal Christian identity, have not in themselves altered Christian doctrines or teachings.

The public, and even many churchmen themselves, seem unaware of the important distinction between doctrines and teachings. Doctrine unfolds the essential divine truths of revelation. It defines the nature of God as disclosed through Scripture and through the tradition of believers whose organic presence is the Church of Christ. Since the Second Vatican

Council the phrase 'the people of God', as a synonym for the Church, has received wide acceptance, and rightly so, for it exactly describes the proper centre of ecclesiology. The 'Church' is the accumulated witness of all those, of the past and of the present, of eternity and of time, whose maintenance of the truth is guaranteed through Christ's promise of the Holy Spirit – 'even the Spirit of truth'. They are a people, not a philosophical ideal or a set of principles or a moral code. The structures of ecclesiastical authority, which in some ages show a bias towards collegiality and in some others seem more concentrated in the custody of centralized officials, are all ultimately dependent on the witness of the whole people of God for the authentication of true doctrine.

Doctrines were finally allowed to crystallize into fixed verbal definitions at the Seven General Councils of the Church held between the fourth and the seventh centuries, and are regarded as immutable. The most elementary scholarship, of course, will show how the proceedings of these bodies reflected the conditions of their age and the transient preoccupations of their participants; it will indicate the pervasiveness of the Greek love of subtle categorizing, for Christian doctrine was established in a thoroughly Greek mental climate. Thus did Providence marry the unique revelation made by God through the historical destiny of the Jewish people to the most seminal intellectual culture the world has ever known. Doctrines once made may never be changed. It is a matter of universal Christian controversy whether or not they may be added to.

The Protestants and the Orthodox suppose that the work of the early Councils was all-sufficient, but within Western Catholicism the doctrine of the Church itself allows that the people of God may receive continuing effusions of revelation. As discussed by such as Mohler, or Franzelin, or Newman, the concept of a 'development' in religious doctrine – a concept implicit in even the earliest Christian scholarship, like that of St Vincent of Lerins in the fifth century – envisages tradition as being slowly unfolded, over centuries, until doctrines are drawn out of the belief of the faithful. The Catholic Church is possessed of the capacity to summon general Councils, and at these such developments may receive formal definition. There were, as it happened, none at the Second Vatican Council; but at the First, in 1870, the infallibility of the Papacy was defined. The notion of development is an explanation of the complicated relationship between faith and human culture, and allows for the part taken by historical change in the reception of ideas and symbols. For its operation there has to be a clearly understood doctrine of the Church, an agreement among believers themselves about the manner in which the truth was entrusted to them, and an appreciation of the extent to which it is inseparable from their own identity. The truth and the means by which it is conveyed, that is to say, are the same. Such conditions do not exist within Protestantism, whose understanding of Christian truth is accordingly more atomistic. These differences over the doctrine of the Church itself are fundamental. They are the rock upon which ecumenical endeavours always founder.

Teaching is quite different. The teachings of the Church are obviously drawn from the applications of doctrine, but they are recognized as being contingent. In relating truth to circumstances all kinds of considerations about the condition of society and the state of human culture need to be evaluated. Here there is recognition that all things are in a process of change, that the life of mankind upon the earth has been characterized by successive forms and ideals, each one of which, naturally enough, has seemed to its enthusiasts to be the final expression of things, beyond further need of adjustment, but each one of which has nevertheless been adjusted and has in the end passed away. How little that today seems to us to survive from the past in reality does so. What we receive and make use of is an image of the past, an image of our own devising, which serves the ends of the present.

Consider the supposed timelessness of traditional worship. The Catholic Mass in the Latin rite, whose recent abandonment is so lamented by traditionalist Catholics, was in large measure (in its external form, not, of course, in its spiritual substance) full of resonances of the Italianate Ultramontane pietism of the nineteenth century. Anglican worship, too, was manufactured by medieval revivalists of the same era, whose rediscovery, as it seemed to them, of the Gothic age as the age of authentic Christian faith, filled the churches with furnishings which are the ones we now so easily regard as permanent expressions of faith.

Political forms, moral ideals, social structures and traditions of authority within society: all are in a condition of more or less permanent mutation. There were perhaps epochs of the past when the processes of change were for a time arrested, or at any rate were disguised from recognition by contemporaries. The nature of modern society precludes recurrences. The universal provision of education, the raised expectations of the world's population, the continued disintegration of traditional society in those parts of the planet where it has managed to persist, the technological change, the crises of culture, the exhaustion of material resources – all point to the improbability of settled conditions in the future of mankind. Christian teachings will inevitably change in order to accommodate the impending transformations, as they have changed in response to differing social patterns in the past. It is the duty of the people of God to see that the doctrines of the faith, however, are preserved intact, for they are the ultimate standard against which all the alterations of teaching and discipline are made.

Let any who doubt that this is the fact of Church teachings ponder how they have adapted to circumstance in the past. The Church has always, for example, insisted on the obligation of believers to obey the civil authorities, and has only allowed the right of rebellion in very special circumstances. In general monarchy was taught as the proper human representation of the divine governance. Today there is widespread Christian consent to the idea that non-democratic governments may be legitimately disobeyed, particularly if they are, as in recent history, colonialist ones. Weighty Christian bodies, like the World Council of Churches, have accordingly encouraged armed resistance movements. Or consider past Christian teachings in relation to fornication or to fasting. In both there have been very extensive adjustments. Society now accepts as perfectly legitimate expressions of human sexual conduct which once were regarded as grossly immodest; so the Church also accepts them. The rules of Christian fasting have virtually disappeared. The place of women in society was the subject of very precise Christian teaching in the past. Its legacy still troubles those concerned with the elimination of sexism.

The relationship of faith and culture, the dialectic of the Church and the world, continues regardless of how strong Christian belief may be at any given time. Sometimes the Church will add more to human culture than it receives; sometimes it will find itself extensively moulded by secular conditions and attitudes. Christianity continues to operate within society's expectations, even when it is critical of those expectations for seeking wrong priorities. To be outside society has seemed a noble ideal to the few who have sought a return to the purity of the desert, but for the generality who bear the responsibility of Christian witness within society the faith can only be meaningful in the available categories of social exchange.

Yet Christians differ radically among themselves about the nature of change. Some have an emotional resistance to any kind of adjustment – generally, although they are scarcely aware of it, because of anterior suspicion of the leadership who are seeking to bring it about. In some cases they could be right. Some believe in not rocking the boat. The leadership of the Western Churches at the present day is rather given to manipulation and to management, hoping to avoid controversy by contriving forms of words that can accommodate widely differing opinions and beliefs. Thus everything can be left alone whilst simultaneously an appearance of activity is created. They are the true conservatives. Some want extensive and fundamental change. These are they whose impatience with what they regard as traditional forms is just as emotionally based as the attitudes of the traditionalists themselves, but whose self-image is that of detached harbingers of a religious faith that accommodates the science-based modules of contemporary culture. They have little sense of the Church as an organic entity, and scant desire to listen to the wisdom of the past as containing truths which transcend the forms in which they are expressed. They are often prepared to alter doctrines as much as teachings, having little comprehension of the difference between them.

It is not surprising that those outside the Church, or upon its periphery, find the whole matter of adaption to the world a stumbling-block. The prospects for controversy are enormous, and the divisions which have opened up within the Churches, between those prepared for change and those resistant to it, are much wider, and just as damaging, as traditional differences over ritual or style ever were. And they should be, too. For these are matters of real substance that involve the doctrine of the Church itself; they are about the nature of the authority by which truth is known to be true. Since there is no way of resolving the differences – as there never is when really important matters are in dispute – believers are asked to put up with the unideal. Depth of feeling on religious issues, issues which engage the whole of the personality, is such that many are unprepared to do so. Impatience with the Churches because of their internal divisions fails to recognize that any worthwhile ideal always divides its adherents, whether it is a political ideology or an aesthetic movement. Ecumenism was until recently the resort of those seeking to end the divisions; now it is increasingly realized that the divisions over the nature of change are as great inside each denomination as they are between the Churches. It is a time for prayer.

11
The Problem of People

It is the weight of intellectual reservation that is usually emphasized by those seeking to explain the decline of Christianity in Western society, but in general, it is the behaviour of Christians themselves which most puts people off. This is either some incorporative impression that the Church does not match up to the ideals it professes (and there is much ransacking of the past to find Christians involved in distasteful enterprises, such as the Inquisition, or the treatment of subject peoples during colonialist rule), or, more probably, an unhappy personal experience in which an individual's understanding of how Christianity should express itself in practice has clashed with a clergyman or someone else in the local church. Similarly with entry to the Church in the first instance: most are attracted not by argument but by example. Most find Christian truth attractive through admiration for particular Christian lives. In any event the result is to place a fearful responsibility upon believers, and it is one they are unlikely to fulfil satisfactorily.

This is partly because the ideal of Christianity entertained by the observer may not be authentic. Christians are sometimes criticized for not adhering to all kinds of moral positions or personal dispositions which may not actually be Christian at all, but are just part of the ill-defined deposit of contemporary humanism. Modern Christians, furthermore, are so poorly informed about their own faith that they are as likely as external observers to produce inaccurate criticism of the behaviour of other believers. Especially today, when the diminished sense of any sort of religious authority allows Christians to construct their own understanding of the faith, there is an enormous area of Christian interpretation which lacks general agreement. The age, which is strangely insistent on uniform moral attitudes over social and political morality, is scornful of authority seeking to lay down precise moral rules in relation to personal conduct, and there is, in consequence, hostility to the notion that Christian allegiance involves subscription to recognized teachings laid down by the Church.

People are, again, put off Christianity because it has sometimes seemed to be an affair of constraints, and this despite the liberal sense of many of today's leaders of religious opinion. There is at the present a renewed emphasis on a return to 'traditional' moral values by the Church, especially by those censorious about the liberal tone of the leadership, but in practice this is only linked to actual doctrinal belief by a relatively small band of Christian traditionalists and Evangelical Protestants. For the most part advocates of moral clarity are much more concerned with enlisting the Church as an agent of social discipline. Should the Church begin to re-emphasize its moral rules – as, for example, over divorce – there would be considerable resistance. It all depends on the issue selected, and on how significantly individuals can allocate moral blame in areas of conduct in which they regard themselves as free of taint.

People look to the Church to stand up for what they regard as moral values, but the content of individual understanding of moral law actually shows great diversity, and so places the Church in an impossible position. It is required to uphold a morality which has no objective acceptance, for it is the projection of individual preference. Yet very large numbers of potential adherents are lost to the Church because they sense that the Church is either not emphatic enough about moral law, or, on the contrary, too emphatic a guardian of outmoded moral discipline. Again consider divorce: the historic Western churches do not allow it, although their members seek divorce in considerable numbers. Some think the Church's teaching on divorce is simply out of touch with social reality, or is insensitive to the suffering germane to destructive marital relationships. Others believe the Church's stand is right, and that it is not insistent enough on its own teaching. In both cases it is not the Church or Christianity which is really under scrutiny – it is individual understandings of what the Church and the community of believers should be like.

The Church has a membership which comprises a pretty even cross-section of human society. Infant baptism secures a technical membership in which even personal choice takes no part. Of the working membership of adult adherents, and of those who look to Christianity as being in some sense the basis of their aspirations to spirituality, the absence of social pressures for religious adherence in the Western world means that the Church is voluntary and self-selected. There are no particular human types: people of all kinds are within the fold of the Church. For some religion is the repository of psychological needs which might as readily have found a niche elsewhere; for some the structure of their personalities finds in religious discipline the best means by which order and shape can be achieved in daily living; some are attracted by sacred theatre, and others by the warmth and companionship they hope to discover in church organizations; some arrive at faith through the observation of Christian lives.

The non-religious reasons for which people adopt a religious identity, which is the staple of the sociology of religion – the intellectual discipline which has made the most important advances in the understanding of religious phenomena in recent times – are now generally seen to include the aspirations to personal identity of the socially marginalized and the socially disorientated. The growth of black sectarian churches in the cities of the Western world illustrates the point. In the end, religion in post-traditional society seems to appeal most through the conditioning of human personality, and the particular style of religion adopted seems to reflect the accidents of personality. In controlled societies, for example, the members of youth organizations (like the Pioneers in the former Soviet hegemony) find just the same sort of moral uplift, personal discipline, sense of purity, and general integration, that members of churches derive from their religious allegiance. Puritans are puritan whatever the outlets available; and types of personality will find expression in hugely varying contexts.

Because Christianity and the world are so closely mixed together, the observer should not be surprised that the spiritual treasure, in earthen vessels after all, is not usually recognizable for what it is at first glance. Adherents of the faith are attracted by example rather than argument: but the example often lacks objective reality – the Christian life which attracts is frequently an invention of the observers' own desire to find something noble to which adherence can be given. Christian lives which become cults, either of the past or of the present (whether Francis of Assisi or Oscar Romero), are so overlaid with propagandist piety that they become artefacts of ideology rather than human realities. People simply do not want to see the living tissue behind the icon. Thus when revelations began to be made about the private life of Martin Luther King many would not believe them. Others found their veneration of Luther King greatly diminished. Now this particular instance gets near to the centre of the question. Luther King was a great Christian because of his spirituality; his lapses from conventional Christian morality are human blemishes – they do not make him any less a great Christian. No one with any wisdom, or any insight into the nature of religious faith, should be put off Christianity because believers do not live up to their own standards. Sometimes, of course, that will be because the standards, anyway, are wrongly understood; sometimes Christian teaching needs adaptation to changed circumstance. But in general the discrepancy between actual living believers and the demands of their religion is normal.

In Christianity the adherent's belief does not transcend his human nature, which is subject to Original Sin, or the accidents of personality – though the latter may be more effectively controlled through precisely the same kind of human psychological mechanics which generate disciplined personalities in ideologically demanding secular societies. Jesus came into the world to save sinners. Those who call upon him do not cease to be as they are: being born again, as Nicodemus was told, means acceptance of the changed status that comes with membership of Christ's Kingdom. The grace of the Holy Spirit does not suddenly eliminate the facts of human nature and the conditioning of circumstance – the accumulation of numerous accidents of personality, most of the decisive ones, furthermore, received at an early age when the individual's role in the formation of personality was involuntary. The Holy Spirit preserves the believer in all truth. The Spirit germinates the seed of faith in spite of the unpromising soil of human personality. After entry into Christ's Kingdom individual believers will continue to behave humanly; they will show the effects which living in the world always shows. Those who enter the Church come into a society of ordinary beings, whose understanding of the faith itself, let alone of matters like right conduct or sensitivity to the needs of others, is alloyed to their humanity. Those who are deterred from religious belief because of the behaviour of religious people are simply deterred by life itself.

Sin is a fact of human nature. Sin is also pretty evenly distributed, so that those whose lives externally appear relatively free of it are nevertheless internally burdened. Religion is not about making a sinless world, or even about the emancipation of individuals from sin. It is about emancipation from the consequences of sin. It is about Christ's free gift of redemption, of forgiveness of sin; so that the sins of individual believers do not impede their progress in spirituality. The fact of sin, and the diversity of human types who constitute the Church, means that those who join in the life of religious associations bring with them the normal accompaniments of human corruption. No one observing the behaviour of Christians should expect to find normal human life suspended. Inside the Church, as outside it, all kinds of people behave in all kinds of ways. Cruelty and ambition and insensitivity, and whatever else most seems to deny the great love of God, are all to be encountered within the society of the redeemed, whose only definition is that they are people who are forgiven by Christ.

The great truths of Christianity were delivered by Jesus, in simple forms and with the imagery of humble lives, to *people*: they were not entrusted to a philosophical system, or to a theoretical understanding of the world, or (as in some Eastern religions) to states of mind. States of mind cannot be achieved by some, and systems of ideas may not be attained by others, and anyway pass from the world with the effluxion of time. Jesus did not even commit his eternal message to a written text. He spoke directly to people, the ordinary people 'who heard him gladly', and prepared a few to go out into the world and convey his truth generally. The few have continued his work ever since. States of mind and ideas may be honed to shape, they have a certain detachment; but the human personality is unpredictable. In giving himself to people Jesus nonetheless made himself relate to people most directly. Yet there are hazards, the hazards of human nature. Among them is the human hope of perfection in an imperfect human environment. It makes many impatient of a religious belief which is accessible to the imperfect – to the imperfection perceived in other people, that is to say. But God calls us as we are, not as we would like to be.

12
Signs of God

'No man has seen God at any time.' That was not a cause of disquiet to most people in the ancient world. Indeed the majesty and supremacy of the divine was precisely why God was not imagined as dwelling in the world he had made, and over which he ruled from a distance. The divine presence, for the ancients, could inhabit images, or signal existence through the special consecration of particular locations, like rivers and mountains. Whether as a pervasive spirit or as a person, the perception of God was always of a mysterious entity, of the ultimately unknowable, who, like the gods of the Greeks, both did and did not communicate with mankind. Their intentions needed to be interpreted, for when they did communicate it was through ambiguous signs, like the configuration of leaves or the flight of birds. The altars of gods were dangerous places, since there the familiar world of men came close to the mysterious forces of the unseen world. Heraclitus said that the god of the oracle at Delphi, Apollo, 'neither speaks nor hides; he indicates'.

The Greeks did not believe in their gods in the way a modern person might believe in Christ: they acknowledged their existence. The modern yearning for religious certainty, for a world in which God is actually visible, was the last thing the ancients would have found conducive, since that would bring the terrifying power of the divine within immediate range, and so, incidentally, remove free-will from men and a great deal of meaning from their time upon the earth. Ancient religion, of course, showed all kinds of variations, and was usually very much more sophisticated than is often thought by modern interpreters, whose crude demythologizing is a prelude to dismissal when it comes to religious phenomena. But all ancient religion disclosed God as, in some sense, mystery: it was the divine force which explained the way the world was, the visible absence of God indicated his sovereignty. He was greater than man, and there was therefore no reason men should be able to see him. 'The wind blows where it will', Jesus said to Nicodemus, 'you hear the sound of it, but you do not know where it comes from, or where it is going.' The

Zeus of Dodona made his will known through the rustling of oak leaves as they were disturbed by the wind.

Modern people are impatient of mystery, and seek not only the closest explanation of the mechanics of things but an understanding of ultimate realities as well. The latter is not available. High in priority among the difficulties that contemporaries have with religious belief is the apparent absence of God from the world. If he is really there, they seem to say, why can we not see him? It is a question with a peculiarly modern urgency. Some settle for an updated Deism. Their understanding of God is of one who has wound up the creation, like a clock, and then removed himself from it; their difficulty is to explain how such a divine force can be known about at all in any personal manner. Some others accept the idea of special revelation. They see that God can have made himself known to his people through a particular tradition or culture; their difficulty is that different traditions and cultures disclose comparable myths about the divine. Which is true? Still others can accept that the God of the Judaic–Christian dispensation is authentic, but believe that the works of men have overlaid the original revelation with an unnecessarily elaborate structure of human interpretation.

The *specific* nature of revelation worries the modern mind as well. Religion somehow has to be large and general, but the divine actually made himself apparent in very precise locations, in the traditions of small groups of people. There is paradox here. For the ancients this very concrete location of the divine was essential for authenticity; a force or a spirit which was too general could not be known about. For modern people it is the general which appeals, and they are sceptical of claims to truth which seem too closely related to precise developments in human culture. They want their God to be, as it were, unsullied by the relative. It troubles them that the history of the Jewish people lacks unique qualities. Here was a people whose trauma in exile, on two historical occasions, elicited the drama of national redemption which defined their God; whose moral code, on close scrutiny, shows all the signs of being the product of a nomadic environment, fashioned in order to preserve the scarce resource of life itself. The tables of the law, delivered by God himself upon the mountain, turn out to be very much like the laws of other primitive societies. The people of the modern world evidently share with the ancients the idea that religion has to be mysterious;

it is just that they cannot leave the mystery alone, picking away at it in the supposition that it may unravel. When they observe religious phenomena through anthropology, or history, or social science, they begin to devalue what they can explain.

But Christianity is about revelation, and therefore about a God who wanted to make himself known and yet is unavoidably removed by his own divinity. The people of his creation cannot conceive him fully for they are not themselves divine beings. Yet the guidance provided by God through revelation – through the entry of his Son into the world, thereby confirming that the vocabulary and symbolism of human understanding of the divine were correct – summons men and women to a progressive participation in the divine creation through the use of the materials of the world. They were not promised an incorporative and universal understanding of things, and will not achieve it. They were, however, called to explore reality in order to prepare themselves for an eternal existence whose nature, again, is outside the range of human imagination. God is in the world, his presence is in the mountains and the rivers, as the ancients knew, and the revelation of the divine presence does offer men the opportunity of a relationship with him. But men do not have the means of seeing the totality, and they lack the divine powers which would otherwise enable the fragments of their understanding to become the whole substance of God's creative will.

It is historical understanding which probably most disturbs the contemporary pursuit of religious certainty. It was, in fact, historical relativism much more than scientific enquiry which did most to cultivate scepticism in the nineteenth century. For Christianity is an historical religion. God was known in the salvation history of the Jewish people; his Son came into the world at the historical congruence of Jewish, Hellenistic and Roman cultures; his truth was delivered to a people, the Church, whose development occurred thereafter in unavoidable circumstances of historical change. The relationship between faith and culture is plotted through historical sequences, and the Church and the world interacted in a series of national cultures.

History, however, was formerly the creature of ideology: the chronicle of events represented the needs which men had to establish the pedigree of their tradition or their claims to social authority. Today, however imperfectly, historical study achieves insights into the nature of human development whose ideological indebtedness is more subtle and whose conclusions induce relativism of judgement. People used to see the hand of God in history. Today, in general, people do not. The past presents itself as a catalogue of random exchanges, and the explanations of historical development which now commend themselves relate to social or economic or cultural causation rather than to the direct involvement of a divine scheme. Yet Christianity is none the less committed to history, and the history of the Church, whose institutional requirements always implied a close proximity to the structures of authority in the world, is the history of a body of believers who were very much of their times. Where once Christian history was a straightforward account of the triumph of the faith, with a few reservations on the side, like those of Gibbon, it is now properly regarded as inseparably related to development in general. The motives of church leaders, formerly presented in one-dimensional explanations of piety, are now recognized as ambiguously annexed to the cultural mixture of each place and time.

There persists in Christian circles, however, a desire to see the operations of God explicitly in human history. And they are surely there. The difficulty is in isolating them for analysis. Just as the divine, for those who are themselves creatures, cannot be separated from the creation, so God cannot be recognized in the historical processes in ways that are specific enough to satisfy the expectations of contemporary Christians. Those expectations are themselves of varying degrees of sophistication. Some simply want history to prove the findings of religious speculation: thus the second coming of Christ will be on this day or on that, because historical evidence indicates the likelihood. Natural disasters or human catastrophe are, by some, taken to signal the impending termination of historical development itself. More in the mainstream, perhaps, are those who look to history to show how God vindicates goodness and punishes evil; though interpretation here is variable according to the selection of available political or moral preference.

The Bible would at first appear to offer justification for the use of historical understanding in this way. The Bible, in fact, comprises a number of approaches to history, but they are all in an illustrative or symbolical frame of reference. When it comes to the meaning of events in a more incorporate texture of interpretation, the Bible is all about Providence. For those who love God, all things work together for good (Romans 8.28).

The whole of history, therefore, expresses the whole of God's will for mankind, and to isolate the meaning of one sequence is to extrapolate it from the full context of God's creative purpose and so to judge the absolute by the contingent, to take a part for the whole. And the whole cannot be known by men, who can see only the evidences of its presence in the creation. History has real meaning, but since both the 'bad' and the 'good' events are, through the operations of Providence, equally productive of the divine purpose, it is plainly unhelpful to interpret history as a collection of moral tales or as a way of showing how God brings about the triumph or the fall of particular groups of people. Thus a catastrophe is exactly what it is: it is not God's way of punishing or warning peoples, or of testing their faith. History, similarly, is an account of the texture of human development; it is the arena in which the truths of revelation are displayed. But it is not the origin of the truths themselves. Modern people have no sense of trust in Providence. Their attempt to explain the mysteries of God amounts, in the end, to a denial of Providence, for it is to discriminate about the utility of experiences instead of recognizing that *all* things work together to achieve the divine purpose. It is, nevertheless, something we all do, and our intellectual values will not allow us to do otherwise.

'The wind blows where it will, and you cannot hear the sound of it.' So are those who are born of the Spirit, Jesus said. It is a powerful image, which corresponds with human experience, but which we never quite find satisfactory. In their urgent pursuit of meaning men and women actually do want to know where the wind comes from and where it is going. Trusting in Providence is compatible with an understanding of the mechanics of things – in this case how the global climate operates. But humanity is never content with the mechanics, and in its restless and creative desire to achieve ultimate explanation it passes beyond the attainable, and faith in Providence slips away. The pursuit itself may have noble qualities, and human life is enriched by the processes of learning. Religion, however, has traditionally insisted that meaning must be sought in the context of belief in the divine purpose. When that does not occur, as in most contemporary intellectual endeavour – where value-prejudice at the outset of enquiry is regarded as improper, but where it nevertheless inevitably happens – the prospect of discerning God in the outcome is slight. But truth is not advanced by the suppression of enquiry. A doctrine of Providence overcomes the difficulty by positing simple trust. It assures men that the phenomena of the natural and the human world are all evidences of the divine presence, wherever intellectual enquiry may lead, and whatever the evidence of historical development may suggest. There is a lyrical moment in Renoir's film *Partie de campagne* where the wind catches the leaves of the trees by a river bank – the symbolism of the wind again. In this case it is witness to the pathos of human love. In the image as used by Christ it is the confirmation of things unseen.

13
God in the Image of Men

It is often said, by people in search of personal or cosmic meaning, that all religions are effectively the same. By this, of course, they mean that the divine - often envisaged as an ethical force or a universal source of life, rather than as a person - visits human experience in a range of ways, and that local cultural conditioning, rather than the nature of the truth itself, provides the differences. So there is seen to be one God, and in their various ways Christ, the Buddha, Mohammed and Krishna, are equally to be esteemed as valid facets of his reality. There is probably little harm, and perhaps even some good, in that. For the inclination to relativize religion does actually incorporate the great truth that God is present to the minds of all people at all times, and that the means by which men and women may recognize him are naturally textured by the circumstances of their environment and culture. But there are also many dangers.

The divine is known first through the created order; in the natural realm God is disclosed to human senses and lays out a geography of holiness which may be recognized by all with eyes to see. This knowledge, however, is formal, latent. Every part of the creation was set in place by God, and the experience of each presents God to human vision. No experience of the created order can furnish evidence that he is not, because there is no other world to stand upon by which this one may be critically evaluated - and this is only one expression of the divine mind. Though sufficient of itself, Christians believe, to enable the peoples of the earth to envisage God, this latent knowledge does not activate a programme of salvation. The religious experiences of the different creeds often elicit sequences of great beauty and of moving human insight, but people remain unredeemed - at the level of formal understanding.

Christianity, on the other hand, is the fruit of revelation: its knowledge of the divine moves beyond the descriptive and beckons men and women to receive forgiveness. Revealed truth is particular and precise: it is God making himself and his will known in detailed historical events - the life of Christ - and it needs to be learned and put into effect for its nature to become apparent. Revelation is active, therefore, in the process of salvation, and promises the deliverance of those who acknowledge their sinfulness. Those aspirants to eternity remain, after admission to Christ's Kingdom, with all their human characteristics, and with the deadweight of Original Sin operating to keep them, still, very much of the earth. Yet they have become – the word 'elected' has the wrong associations to modern ears – designated as citizens of an everlasting city, their spiritual status changed. And Christian believers are poor indeed as witnesses to the celestial splendour that has fallen upon them; blinkered by the passions inseparable from human existence their frailty incapacitates the vision offered to the humblest and the most ignorant. It is the oldest of religious paradoxes: those who are poor in the trappings of human society became rich in the treasury of sanctification. 'Silver and gold have I none,' Peter said to the lame man at the gate, 'but such as I have I give you.'

Revelation is particular in that it relates to a given people at a moment of cultural development, and it is also exclusive. Nothing is so unacceptable to the modern temper as religious exclusivity – rendered as doctrinal exactitude. But doctrine and dogma are the necessary accompaniments of revealed truth; they are verbal definitions of the particularization of the divine. That is, again, alien to the expectations of modern men and women, who prefer religious truth to be general. The truths of Christianity, located in the Judaic spiritual culture of the Roman period in Palestine, seem to them to be merely relative. When other religious traditions are examined, *their* precise location appears equally valid to the modern observer – who can discern no reason to prefer one to the other.

This relativizing of religious phenomena fits well with the contemporary veneration of humanity, and is of the same kind of belief as the universalism of salvation, the priority of morality over spirituality, and the equation of human goodness with God's love. The piety of today requires people to declare that they love humanity. But no one can love humanity: it is too various, too general, and too vague a concept. It is possible to love individuals, and perhaps some of the associations into which they are drawn for the purposes of social continuity. There is an end of it, however. With religion the same threshold operates. No one can love or even know a God who is so universal and so given to indiscriminate intimations of his presence that all people at all times are equally repositories of his nature.

The whole point about the Christian doctrine of the incarnation is that God became a man in order to be comprehended by men in ways which presaged their individual salvation. The universal was made particular, within the cultural forms of a people whose own preceding salvation history had furnished the models and fashioned the moulds which gave the coming of God into the world precise meaning. When religion is made so general that it incorporates all experience men have of the divine presence it ceases to be active for men and becomes, indeed, a simple return to descriptive natural truth. Then men and their environment become inseparable, and religion returns to its most primitive renditions – a version of animism, dignified, in the modern world, with symbols derived from secular tributes to human inventiveness. Thus religion is said to stem from 'man's quest for truth', or from his 'moral sense'. Whether the finished product is packaged as Krishna or Christ scarcely matters; the great thing is that humanity has signalled the discovery of its own serious potential for knowledge. The face of God discerned within the different cultures is regarded as a human contrivance. The divine reality which lies behind it is so broad and indiscriminate as to encompass the totality of all human anticipations of moral seriousness.

The scene has shifted some way from the condemnations of 'Indifferentism' made by the Roman Catholic Church in the nineteenth century. When Pius IX denounced this liberal dogma in his *Syllabus of Errors* in 1864, it was thought that the fault occurred when Christians of the day claimed that differing traditions of Christianity (as between Catholic and Protestant) were inessential matters. Today traditionally minded Christians are hard put to it in persuading their own co-religionists that theirs is a version of God superior to that held out in Buddhism or Hinduism. Eastern religions, in particular, have enjoyed a great vogue since the nineteen-sixties, when intellectuals and their clients managed to ignore the traditional social ethics of the major religions (cleaned up by contact with Christian values in colonial times) in order to praise their spiritual insights. Interestingly enough, this development took place at exactly the same time that Christianity was being vilified in the West for its poor social record. It was noticeable, then as now, that the 'spiritual' qualities admired in the Eastern religions were those which enhanced individual lives and gave them purpose and direction – and thus indirectly flattered human qualities – and that those elements most rejected in Christianity were the ones which aspired to other-worldliness and asceticism. Indiscriminate respect for world religions, and associated criticism of Christianity, is the most unhelpful contemporary version of 'Indifferentism'. The fears of Pius IX, expressed, as may now be seen, with such moderation, were certainly justified.

The authentic insights of the world religions, on the other hand, and the moving human sensibilities which they elicit, have enormous potential for the enrichment of Christianity. In that sense a multi-faith consciousness may be very advantageous. It also encourages mutual respect between religious confessions and the different ethnic groups who are their devotees, and that, also, can only be a gain. But the perspective for Christians needs to be right: it is a matter of adding new dimensions to a clearly maintained body of doctrines, and so observing how they may flower more vigorously in the enriched soil of what once was very improperly regarded as alien terrain.

Instead of that, however, the present mood casts all religions into the melting-pot. The artefact which emerges resembles the human form, for it is a god made in the image of men's sensations, suited to the religion of humanity, indiscriminate in its affections, undemanding in its spiritual requirements, but extremely exacting when it comes to social ethics or political morality. Its creators are good people, seeking an accommodation with prevailing values: their intentions are fine but the results of their labours are lamentable, for they are religious illiteracy. When modern Westerners encounter truly demanding religion – as in the Islamic revival – they are horrified. It dares to dictate the terms upon which men and women are to live out their existence; it speaks to its followers of the exclusive demands and religious observances of daily life. It is, in short, religion. That it is, in the judgement of some, not very agreeable religion, is all the more reason for resistance to the notion that all religions are essentially the same. Rather than countenance the dismantling of their temple of human values, however, Westerners prefer to write off the Islamic revival as a species of fanaticism, not properly eligible for inclusion in the canons of their universal church.

Generalizing religious truth flatters contemporary intellectual assumptions. If religion is to be believed at all by educated opinion, it must apparently match the cultural relativity of other attitudes. Only those things may be regarded as acceptable which correspond to universal human qualities. These inevitably turn out to be moral rather than spiritual – though it is now conventional for them to be described, along with aesthetic appreciation, as characteristics of 'the human spirit'. People in all cultures, so this line of thought suggests, share great human aspirations and rights, which may be identified and categorized. The governments of the world, to receive moral sanction, must recognize them, and the place of religion is to sacralize them. Hence the religion of humanity, to which the official Christianity of today is increasingly showing many affinities. It is one thing to say that the divine is in all the great religions of the world – and an important thing to say as well – but it is quite another to equate the religions and to regard truth as evenly distributed among them. Those whose religious sense is satisfied by such a conclusion naturally find the exclusivity of traditional Christianity distasteful. They go on to see it as uneducated, too. For the people of vision, so they imagine, are those who realize that God is one, in the way that mankind is one, and that the different cultures have merely represented him in unnecessary and disposable variations.

When all religious experience is perceived to be the same the demands of God become so general as to be virtually without meaning. A universal religiosity may appeal to the intellectual temper of the times, but it leaves the actual need of the individual for religious understanding incapable of adequate fulfilment. It is no accident that the arrival of a universal and ethicized God has signalled, also, the descent of religious emptiness upon those who have acclaimed the new truth. The divine cannot be known as a person when he is represented in the symbols of a universal brotherhood of men, for the general is too general to have a possible individual application. The spiritual desolation of the Western world is the more searing because its victims are progressively less and less knowledgeable about the religious tradition they have abandoned, and so have nothing to recover. Fragmentary recollection of childhood faith, like the last fragrant memories of a departed friend, still haunt the imagination and prompt nostalgic regret for the receding beauty. The prevailing sense of loss is always knocking on the door of human consciousness; the sound diminishes, however, as the particular is displaced more and more persistently by the general. Very soon men and women will have nothing left to recall: there will be no distant resonances of the discarded faith.

14
What is Worship?

There is a problem about worship. For the unchurched masses in Western society – people who have no connection with institutional religion, yet who none the less are insistent that they are in some sense Christian believers – worship has little meaning. They may say their prayers, and it would be an impertinence to enquire into what that means to them; but the probability is that they comprise simple petitions for relief from the misfortunes of life. Of worship itself their lives are untouched: there is no secular counterpart in modern society of which religious worship could be considered a sanctified version. Worship engages the whole natures of men and women and, because they are a complex of attitudes and reflexes, it strikes many resonances. First in importance, however, is surely the effect which authentic worship has in evoking the divine presence on earth. It is, in that sense, a cultic exercise. It is the way in which a people who are initiates into the mystery of Christ's divinity encounter him in sequences which are unlike the normal experiences of daily living. Though religious truth does not depend upon subjective experience, and is independent of our wills or intellects, religious worship is presented through emotion: the believer needs an evocation of the divine presence, and for that he brings the whole of his being, mind and spirit, into the assembly of a heavenly drama.

Worship is thus very special. It uses the cultural materials of the world in order to dematerialize existing reality, so that the truths of the celestial order may be perceived and the unknowable mysteries of God encountered in a sacred theatre where they can be illustrated. The visible materials of worship have necessarily to correspond with human experiences of the present life. In traditional society worship depended heavily on the forms of earthly authority for the images – God presided over his people as a civil ruler ordained the arrangements of a hierarchical society. The heavenly mysteries descended to the earth as liturgical formulae cultivated in the believer a transformed version of earthly authority and made it visible to men. The spatial limitations of human understanding, at the same time, could be considered as transcended by miraculous occurrences to material things: bread and wine became, again, the very elements of Christ's passion, and children dipped in holy water at the font were sealed for ever as Christians. Sacramental worship was obviously the most satisfactory, for it offered truth which was objectively present, independent of the actual thought or moral condition of priest and congregation.

The modern world seemingly has no model of which this understanding of worship is a sanctified version. Secular authority has very properly been asked to explain itself, and the resulting tempered egalitarianism, though not without its counterparts in contemporary Christian worship, is a very unsatisfactory basis for an evocation of the supreme sovereignty of God. Democratic societies are a confederation of discussion groups and committees: God is not best worshipped through the symbolism of majority resolutions. The whole fabric of contemporary Western culture is cerebral and expressed in a series of intellectual categorizations. The religious counterpart of that is a strong tendency for worship to become an affair of reading from a book – rather than of following a rite performed in gestures and liturgical representations intended to convey timeless truths. Recognizing the need for worship to be, as they would say, a rich emotional experience, modern Christians turn instead to sequences of music, or drama or dance, in order to express their beliefs. This has a limited effectiveness, and may also be rather identifiable in social class terms. Religious traditionalists have been much disturbed by the use of contemporary language in the liturgy. It is not clear that language itself matters all that much, in the kind of issues being raised here, for individuals soon begin to invest their spiritual sense in any style of language. The purposes of worship, disclosed through the symbolism of uses, are what matter.

The worldly model of which worship is a sanctified representation most employed by the Christians of today is the *community*. Modern Christian worship emphasizes community above all other features. It seeks to evoke the idea of a people meeting in order to encounter the source and directive of their sense of shared values. There are heavy ethicist overtones here, and the extent to which modern Christianity has ethical priorities, rather than spiritual ones, is represented in the rhetoric of human brotherhood, justice, and shared social obligation, which breathe out of much contemporary worship. Even services prescribed in detail by ecclesiastical authority, like the Anglican Holy Communion, or the Catholic Mass, often manage to reflect this emphasis – not, it is true, in the words of the liturgy themselves, but in the symbolism of gestures, like the extended and demonstrative 'kiss of peace'. As a corrective to the cold isolation that could easily describe some of the worship that preceded these exercises, in which the worshippers often seemed unable to share any human warmth, the present tone may be comprehensible enough. But it has developed one understanding of Christianity at the expense of others.

More serious, however, is that the worship is by nature closed. Emphasis on community necessarily creates a separation from those who are outside it, and the unchurched masses, who consider themselves as Christian but who do not go to church, are left further than ever from the centre of their neglected yet still somehow valued ultimate allegiance. Worship as something performed, to which a believer can call in, as it were, and which he or she can find familiar and easy to recognize, because he or she is not required to participate in apparently spontaneous symbolic acts of human brotherhood, known to the regular enthusiast, is less and less available. Worship as an expression of shared community values is not intended to evoke divine mysteries, and it does not do so. Its own valuable representation of an important dimension of the Christian life is, however, unavoidably limiting because it requires a new sort of initiation – into a tightly drawn community of believers.

Thus the modern world does, after all, provide a model for Christian worship. It is the worship of human values. But what of the evocation of the unseen world; where is the sacred theatre which, like baroque illusionism, allows us to penetrate the mysteries of eternity through symbols which relate, not to human values, but to anticipations of the divine order? If worship, in at least one of its modes, used to employ the materials of the earth in order to bring the heavens before the vision of men, where now are the contrivances which may present the believer with something outside normal experience? There are none. The truth is that the materialist culture of the Western world, and the expectations which derive from it, are now so far removed from a spiritual understanding of humanity that there are not enough meeting-points for religion any longer to employ material models in attempts to symbolize sanctification. Instead, churchmen turn to music and the arts to provide what, for them, is an elevating substitute; it has the enormous advantage of prompting emotional responses which bridge the divide between believers and non-believers. All kinds of people can be moved by music, and it will seem as if their finest instincts are engaged. This simulation of worship is now widely mistaken for the real thing. The arts were always employed by the Church in its service; abbots and bishops were once the great patrons of artistic endeavour. In their hands, however, art was used, totalitarian fashion, to propagate truths which were known on independent and superior authority. Now art is thought to supply its own basis for insights into reality. It is self-authenticating, and religious authority does not dare to interfere with its interpretation of truth. The Church no longer employs art: it has been taken over by it.

The problem of worship in modern society remains. People now expect worship to elicit a richly satisfying emotional response, appropriate and suited to their own emotional inclinations. They do not see it as a means of bringing them into the presence of celestial forces quite unlike their own complex needs. Christ is no longer envisaged as a supreme ruler and judge, but as the dispenser of reassurance and human sympathy. The existing version of the divine doubtless has some valuable insights, but is has disintegrating effects on worship. Precisely because worship is now expected to cater for human needs, rather than be a means of bringing humanity out of its preoccupations, it will have to be as various as there are individuals in need. And that cuts across the ideal of worship as community. Each will emphasize some aspect of personal need, some emotional requirement which religion is to meet. A person may find short-term benefit from one particular style of worship, which seems suited to the emotional demands of the moment, but with time it may be superseded by quite other interior impulsions. Hence one of the most distressing characteristics of contemporary Christian worship: its fragile hold on the worshippers. Evidently the slightest distaste for some aspect of the worship of their local church will cause believers to move on to another, or to lapse from public worship altogether. There is no sense of obligation, of the duty of supporting local institutions because they are visible embodiments of universally held truths. People shop around at will, for they have come to regard worship as essentially to do with the satisfaction of emotional demands. In a way this individualizing of worship is understandable. Because religion engages the whole of the personality it is hardly surprising that different aspects of our inner selves will from time to time, or perhaps even simultaneously, direct our emotions in different directions. Seeking different experiences of worship, appropriate to the interior facet most evident at the time, will inevitably make worship an extension of a divided interior life. But the trouble is that modern religion does *not* engage the whole personality. Individuals have so marginalized their spiritual sense, and so confused it with aesthetic and emotional promptings, that they do not bring the whole of themselves into the question of worship. They bring, on the contrary, only one dimension - and that the one which at the time most seems in some sort of human need. Worship then becomes a matter of anodyne enterprise. We need to learn again how to use the symbolism provided by the materials of the world in order to reach out to the eternal divinity who is outside ourselves. Worship is about surrender to a sovereign who is independent of our needs.

15
The Secularization of the Church

Secularization is a more complicated social condition than may at first appear. Social scientists have offered a number of definitions, but for a simple approach let it be agreed that secularization exists where the daily life of individuals and of society is conducted without reference to religion. Plainly the contrast with traditional societies of the past is considerable: then the passage of the season was marked by religious festivals, family life cultivated a discipline of devotion to the saints who would protect the members and secure their passage to eternity through intercession, public life employed religious symbolism as a signal of authority, and the extensive influence of the Church maintained a visible structure of religious dedication for the purposes of human association.

It is easy to romanticize about traditional society. There were many covert unbelievers, there was widespread persistence of pagan rituals and beliefs, and there were doubtless many who used the religious culture for personal ends. But however much an individual may have succeeded in escaping the immediate control of religious sanction he actually lived in a world where mysterious forces were universally acknowledged to hedge the destinies of men and women, and where with the fall of night the agents of evil roamed the countryside. Few doubted the existence of the unseen world, and the passage of time was punctuated with religious observances which made its presence seem close. The supposition that everyone went to church needs adjustment, it is true, since it is evident that even in the most determined 'ages of faith' actual attendance at religious worship was episodic for many individuals. Women have always been more attentive to religious observance than men: in the Catholic culture of Latin American countries, for example, where the pattern of traditional religiosity persisted until only yesterday, it was quite normal for the women to attend Mass and for the men to hang around at the church door towards the end of the service. This customary behaviour, however, occurred in an atmosphere which assumed the truth of religion and expected it to be built into the fabric of family and public life.

The Islamic revival of the present time is showing an unexpected development: the religious observances of a traditional society are being restored within an urban and material culture. Many sociologists had always supposed that secularization and urbanization were closely related, and most intellectuals had imagined that an educated society would progressively abandon religious belief. Even within Christian society, as it happens, there were examples of urbanization co-existing with high levels of religious affiliation – in Poland, South Africa, America and Ireland. In such places, however, it was always thought, by those who thought about it at all, that in due course a rising level of secularization would eventually expunge religious observance. The phenomenon was anyway not always what it seemed. Thirty years ago Will Herberg was contending that the very high levels of religious affiliation in American society were explicable in terms of social integration, and that it was the role of the churches in fostering social identity, rather than in the purveyance of religious doctrines, that accounted for their popularity.

Modern Western society is actually very deeply secularized. That this sometimes appears not to be the case is because there are also many survivals of the former religious confessionalism. In England and in Sweden, for example, there are state Churches with erastian associations still attaching to them, and in Germany provision is made through the taxation system for public support of religion. Many governments provide for chaplains in their armed forces and in some types of state-funded welfare institutions. Symbols of Christianity are still a part of public life – even in the United States, with its long-standing constitutional separation of Church and state, public prayers are offered at the inauguration of a president. In America religion is strictly excluded from the schools aided by government; in England, however, not only is there a legal requirement for the teaching of Christianity in the state schools but there is also generous public funding of denominational institutions. England is perhaps the most secular of those countries which have not had an interlude of Marxist rule in the second half of the twentieth century, yet England has a sovereign who is constitutionally obliged to be a member of the state Church, and to be, indeed, its legal head.

For the fact is that many of these survivals of the close relationship of Church and state which once existed are now highly formal. It would be regarded as a very improper violation of individual liberty if legal endorsement of Christianity had any really practical consequences for daily life. Institutions which publicly profess a religious link are often in reality conducted without reference to Christian beliefs. Church educational foundations, for example, are in many instances more concerned with the maintenance of the same kind of professional standards and values as exist in secular education than they are with Christian doctrine or with the cultivation of specific religious observance. They tend to make appointments to their staffs with minimal enquiry into personal belief. In England the state Church is rarely consulted by government, even when parliament is legislating on moral questions, such as marriage law, which are plainly within the area of ecclesiastical concern. When the Church is consulted it is only as one institution among others, and it is treated as an agency involved with moral issues rather than as the national teacher of moral or spiritual values.

Daily life in Western societies is typically untouched by connection with religion. The household custom of family prayers has long since passed, as has the personal habit of Bible reading. Some of these observances, like family prayers, were anyway social class indicators and characterized sections of the middle class. Religion has now been relegated by the media to a specialist interest, and in discussion programmes on television, in most Western countries, Christianity is treated as a religious phenomenon, along with others, rather than as a vital repository of public values. Most people in all these societies lack any daily acquaintance with transcendence. The nature of life in modern society does not accommodate religious observance, even if individuals felt minded to attempt it, and men and women in a secular culture get what personal uplift they feel they may need from moral concern and from the supposedly elevating effects of aesthetic appreciation. Despite widespread declamations about human values and moral imperatives, most people in fact lead lives which are directed by material considerations, and become absorbed by the infrastructure of social organization.

For Christians the most alarming feature of all ought to be the internal secularization of Christianity itself. This is a controversial matter, but it can plausibly be argued that for many Christians, and for many church leaders, the faith has in recent decades been progressively reinterpreted as a texture of ethicism rather than as a spiritual culture. Christians these days lead lives which are materially untouched by the religious beliefs they simultaneously profess. This is not to imply that they are hypocritical or unfaithful to their trust, but that the manner of living in contemporary society excludes the possibility of expressing religion in a structured fashion. Traditional society was very different. Some truly dedicated people will always manage to associate daily living with religious meaning – with varying degrees of accuracy – but they are increasingly the exception in modern Western society. Our culture is now arranged, like the details of daily life, so that religion has no immediate point of reference. Instead, contemporary culture treats Christianity as a cultural phenomenon of the past, as a way of explaining how the present world of values was once formed. Christians have themselves often come to accept precisely the same attitude in relation to their own religious understanding. The contemporary impatience with dogma (exact doctrine), and the pervasive universalism (eternal life all round) are indications of the way in which secular values have penetrated Christianity. The managerial style of conducting institutions, often necessary for economic considerations or as a means of rationalizing resources, and the associated bureaucratization, have also imported the values of the world into the Church. The styles of committee decision, and the simulations of parliamentary procedure, which now describe the internal government of the churches, all make organized Christianity less distinctive when compared with secular institutions. In prevailing conditions many of these things are perhaps unavoidable: the point is that they add up to a creeping secularization of Christianity itself. Christian discourse is scarcely distinguishable from the secular moralism of the intelligentsia. Its view of human values is their view, and the moral agenda of the world and of the Church is these days usually in agreement.

Some, however, will point to the survival of a kind of 'folk religion' in society. There are, they will say, very many who claim religious belief when prompted by opinion pollsters, or whose hidden Christianity is real enough despite being independent of the churches. A lot of this style of belief, however, is a rapidly disappearing feature of a population which still remembers the Christian hymns and symbols which were universal in the schools of their childhood. The children of today are accumulating much less of a religious deposit on which they may be able to draw in later life. Religion has virtually disappeared from many secondary schools, and a knowledge of the Bible is no longer in any sense part of popular culture. Family life does not usually encourage instruction in religion either. Where public life withdraws more and more from the promotion of religious belief it is the family and the churches which must become more vigilant in compensation. There are no signs that this is happening, and the renewed calls for family values, indeed, emphasize the behavioural advantages of Christian moral teaching rather than the doctrinal structure of Christian spirituality. The values of the contemporary Church are often scarcely separable from secular values, being represented in the same moral rhetoric; and the doctrinal teachings of the Church are frequently observed to be rather imprecise and also rather occasional.

Secularization exists in varying forms in different layers of the social mixture, but its strength is greater than people think. It is a major impediment to Christian belief, for where daily life is largely unaffected by reference to religion, religion itself can scarcely seem important enough to attract belief. And where the churches become so marginalized in society, and Christianity itself becomes so individualized, that their influence is radically diminished, public understanding of the nature of the faith itself will display much ignorance. The days are past when the churches should look to the state, or to social institutions, to propagate Christian truth. The secularization of the state and public institutions may be a necessary consequence of liberal values which are plainly desirable for reasons of social justice. But unless the churches compensate by contriving an effective presence, and promoting a clear message, the spread of Christian truth will not occur.

16
What is the Church?

How well placed are the churches to propagate Christian values and Christian truth without the support, which once they had, of governmental and social institutions? Is the public perception of them and of their role one that has any relation to the reality of their condition, and will it be conducive to the cultivation of religious belief? In these areas there is considerable variation in the different countries of the Western world.

Americans are sometimes very surprised by the degree of hostile criticism of the church leaders which they encounter in the European press. This criticism, however, is of aspects of the churches as institutions, not of religion, and it probably reflects a general sense that the churches are inadequate as guardians of Christianity. Many feel that the churches are too involved with issues of social justice, and are, paradoxically, not religious enough. Much criticism of the Church is unwarranted: people expect ultimate standards to apply in religious institutions, while they only expect relative ones of other social organizations. They suppose that the Church should be perfect, and where they do encounter the imperfections of Christian ministers they expect them to be of the order of amusing little human failings. The more Christian belief is individualized – the more each believer manufactures his own version, corresponding to interior emotional requirements, and innocent of reference to religious authority or tradition – the more chance there is that scorn of the Church, for not sharing the private vision, will grow. There is little sense that truth is guaranteed to the Church as Christ's body on earth, through the operations of the Holy Spirit rather than the capabilities of men and women. People do not see the need for an adequate doctrine of the Church: they see the Church as a collection of believers, not as an eternal corporation whose living members in the world at the present time are a small fraction of the whole. It is the whole which declares the truth, not only the fraction on earth. People also have no sense that truth is independent of the failings of individual churchmen.

The matter is an important one. Christ delivered his message to the whole company of adherents, and it is inseparable from the totality. Outside the Church there is no salvation: the ancient formula still applies today. 'Securus judicat orbis terrarum' – the words of St Augustine, which proved decisive in the religious odyssey of Cardinal Newman, point to the perils of private judgement in matters of religious doctrine. But this is not a concept that appeals to modern observers, whose relativized sense of what constitutes truth has to do with the integrity of the individual, and with emotional satisfaction, and not with the universal witness of the faithful. If they conclude that many adherents of Christianity are unworthy, as not living up to their own professions, then they are reluctant to attribute to them any possession of the truth at all, as part of a wider community of believers. And their definition of unworthiness relates to the highly individualized understanding of Christianity that is regarded as appropriate for thinking people.

Just as the efficacy of the sacraments is independent of the worth of the ministers who arrange them, however – for they are objectively true, and take no vitality from the accidents of human qualities – so the truth given to the Church is independent of individual believers. Yet modern people just do not think in this kind of way. The most commonly used word of approval in contemporary society is 'sincerity'. The clergy are approved of if they are 'sincere'; the religious convictions of others, and their sense of Christian truth, are acceptable if they are 'sincere'. But only a momentary reflection will show that people can be very sincere in their adherence to ideas that are erroneous. Sincerity goes well with relativized and individualized religious faith, for each person can respect the beliefs of others on the strength of human sentiment, and so avoid the painful contemplation of exact doctrine. That the sacraments are independent of the worthiness or otherwise of the ministers who perform them has no great attraction as an idea to those whose sovereign concept is sincerity. If the clergyman is thought to be a humbug, because of some insensitivity or other, the sacraments will be abandoned and the people will seek the satisfaction of their religious sense elsewhere.

It is precisely the same sort of impatience with institutionalized religious authority that makes for populist ecumenism. The theological technicalities which trouble the minds of church leaders relate mostly to their failure to agree about the doctrine of the Church, and ecumenical efforts come apart over this central matter. The difficulties relate to the structure of authority within which the whole company of believers recognize and validate doctrine. But the men and women of today are unconcerned with exact doctrine, and regard religion more as an affair of sentiment and sincerity. There is a very widespread disposition to be scornful of the churches for not sinking their differences and uniting around a number of agreed general propositions. This populist ecumenism actually has resonances within the leadership of the churches themselves, and especially within the Protestant churches, where consciousness of the need for a doctrine of the Church is less evident. Public understanding of the considerations which divide the churches has little to do with processes for the validation of truth, either, and concentrates on another cause of division. This is religious psychology.

Any idea or movement which engages the whole personality will affect individual sensibilities in different ways; it will be a cause of division, that is to say. It is almost a test of the worth of an idea that it will split its adherents into a number of competing understandings and practices. In the case of religion some, for example, like sacred theatre, while others prefer their celebration of truth to be unadorned; some value timeless expressions, and others are moved by spontaneity. The churches are divided by these things, both internally and, more enduringly, in denominational symbols. Though Christian divisions are fundamentally over the doctrine of the Church and consequential matters of authority, it is these issues where differences of spiritual psychology have received institutional expression which most believers regard as important. To those outside the churches the distinction is not apparent, and they cannot find much sympathy for division of any sort.

The churches are also divided by social class phenomena: the 'churches of the disinherited', the flowering of sectarianism at the social margin, and the employment of religious fervour within movements of social reform, are all familiar features of the sociology of religion, and Christian history provides rich evidences of them. Most of the mainstream denominations in the Western world at the present time show signs of being influenced by class characteristics of the bourgeoisie who have for long provided the leadership. For all that, the essential differences between the churches remain centred in matters of authority. The public are unaware of it. They can only see a religion divided by what seem to be quite soluble issues of symbolism and tradition.

The sad truth is that most of those who are outside the Church are very ignorant of religious teachings. There is a widespread assumption that Christian truths are self-evident, and require no specialist understanding. Christianity is recognized as the form in which, for reasons of historical development, the human decencies of the culture are expressed. The essence is helping people. That Christianity is a structure for the comprehension of human wickedness, and a series of disciplines which prepare the believers for initiation into an eternal Kingdom, does not immediately appeal to the Western mind - though these are features which are greatly esteemed in the vitality of Christianity in the developing world.

Western Christians expect their religion to consecrate their existing sense of truth, and goodness, and moral beauty. Their knowledge of the Bible is thin, and their understanding of doctrine slight. It is scarcely surprising that those outside the churches altogether acquire little idea that the Church is a unique repository of truth. This ignorance, fortunately, extends to the internal procedures of religious organization - otherwise they would be deterred still more. Public exposure to the Church, through media reporting, is episodic; it relates to controversial issues or to occasional scandals. No one outside the most committed church circles has much idea of what synods or general assemblies get up to. That is doubtless very salutary. For if the public are impatient of the churches because of what appear to be denominational obscurities, they would indeed find the technical discussions of ecclesiastical bodies quite intolerable, since their view of religion as consecrated welfare precludes any notion that institutional organization is important.

There is a strange contradiction in existing impressions of the Church. The public applauds the moral concern of the clergy, in the same way as they do the moral declamations of a pop star or a politician; but they are sceptical of too much spirituality, in the supposition that it disqualifies the clergy from practical knowledge of the social state. There is also a pervasive prejudice against clerical involvement with political issues - unless, from the perspective of the observer, the political matter involved is in fact not really political but moral. Now contemporary politics has become so moralistic, with the participants and their enthusiasts representing their opinions in the high language of human rights ideology, that virtually the entire range of political debate can be considered as coming within the sphere of religion.

This suits Christian claims, heightened by the indebtedness of church leaders to the secular political culture, that the whole of life in the most detailed aspects is under the sovereignty of God anyway, and cannot properly be separated from the sanctions of religion. Yet the public do not welcome clerical action in the political sphere, correctly regarding the church leadership as no more qualified or competent to make political judgements than anyone else.

The contradiction is this: the church has, or should have, clear teachings on moral issues, and such teachings are in theory exactly what the public expects; but in reality the public does not allow that the religious leadership should get involved with telling them how to behave in moral questions where these questions are matters of political controversy. And that is most questions. So the Church is in the end left with no room to manoeuvre. The public wants moral exhortation without content; it expects the clergy to give a moral lead without actually attaching the Church to structured morality. Whatever the confusions of thought, however, the result is the same: a disinclination to look to the Church as a primary source of moral reference, even by those who regard themselves as being in some sense Christian believers.

All these difficulties, furthermore, are independent of the serious theoretical discussions about the propriety of religious morality receiving the endorsement of law in the political arrangements of a society of plural values. They are difficulties which are much more on the surface, made by people poorly acquainted with the doctrines of Christianity and with the effects of false consciousness in political choice. The individualizing of religious interpretation by the clergy themselves, in their attempts to fashion a version of the Christian faith compatible with the intellectual and social needs of contemporary society, complicates matters still further, since it, also, diminishes the possibility that the Church will be able to represent itself as a coherent witness to agreed truth. If the general criticisms of the Church are often founded on insecure data, it must be conceded that the officers of the Church themselves do not help public acceptance of Christianity when they are unable to express their beliefs consistently. 'There are two kinds of writers,' Raymond Chandler once said, 'writers who write stories, and writers who write writing.' Churchmen tend to be found in the second category.

17
Questions of Sexual Morality

There are considerable numbers of Roman Catholics in Europe and North America who believe that their Church's teachings on sexual ethics are too traditionalist. During papal visits to countries in those areas there were even demonstrations by liberal Catholics seeking changes in the official teachings. The trauma following the renewed condemnation of artificial means of birth control, in the encyclical letter *Humanae Vitae* (1968), has continued to make many question the basis of quite a wide range of Catholic teachings on ethical matters. Many others simply ignore the teachings in practice, while continuing a general adhesion to the Catholic Church. With Anglicans the position is reversed. Here there are many who believe that the leadership is too liberal, and there are increasingly calls for a return to traditional certainties in questions of personal morality. The re-emergence of the Evangelicals as the most dynamic element within the Church of England, after almost a century of domination by the High Church and the Broad Church, also clearly reinforces inclinations towards traditional moral values – which they see as the moral code of the Bible. There are thus powerful influences within the Western churches which pull in opposite directions on these issues, and those outside Christianity, who are contemplating its appeal, can shop around. There are many who turn away from a religious allegiance which may seem to condemn what they are or what they have done: homosexuals, for example, or those who have been divorced. There are also many who adhere to the Church precisely because of its guardianship of moral certainty, and who took to it for the maintenance of what are now usually referred to as 'family values'.

The Church is involved in judgements about human sexuality for a very obvious reason: the Bible has a lot to say about it, and since sexual relationships are concerned with the stewardship of others they are one of the most common forms in which people encounter personal moral choice. Because sex and procreation are linked, the divine gift of life itself is part of the reason why religion has necessarily always insisted on the priority of moral teaching. Religion is also the repository of primitive folk wisdom, and rules governing sexual relationships recall distant needs of the fragile existence of nomadic peoples, needs for preserving life and so for the outlawing of sexual actions which might inhibit the possibility of conception and birth.

Sexuality was once regarded as one-dimensional, it was a matter of keeping the race going; now it is recognized as a spectrum of impulses and responses which may affect the person in several different ways simultaneously. The simple polarization of male and female is too simple: there are enormous numbers of individuals for whom sexual identity has some grey areas. Modern understanding of how the mind operates – the revolution in attitudes brought about by psychology – has shown a complex congruence of thought and sexual impulse which forbids easy assessment in precise categories. The teachings of the Church must take account of these and other developments, and especially of social developments which have produced a context in which the sexual behaviour of men and women has shifted radically from the fixed and codified norms of traditional society.

In traditional society the supply of children maintained group loyalties and identities. The family, the village community, the tribe, needed sexual practices compatible with a high birth-rate. The economy of human life was wasteful: high infant mortality and the relatively short life-span of adults required frequent births in order to sustain society. The socializing of children took much less time than it does today, when young adults do not even leave educational institutions until they are more than a decade and a half old. There was then only a few years in which the young population could receive its conditioning in the values of society, and as there was virtually no educational provision which could associate moral law with cultural ideals the moral code was exclusively religious, and was necessarily expressed in precise terms which left no room for personal judgement or choice, or for relative assessments of different sexual practices. In primitive society morality thus became an affair of exact definitions, consecrated by the authority of religious belief. It was supposed that the will of God sanctioned the rules of behaviour, not the requirements of social organization.

Now from the religious perspective God's will is always the sovereign consideration when seeking an explanation of sexual morality; but it is unclear in the conditions of modern society and modern knowledge that God's will and social necessity can be as easily equated today as once they were. The more that is learned about human biology, and about the relative nature of social organization, the more it must seem that the subtlety of human impulses suggests a subtle moral framework, rather than a series of flat rules.

At this point traditionalist moral guardians observe that liberal morality is really just a surrender to human moral frailty. But that is not a sound conclusion. Men and women are called to submit to God's laws – there are no grey areas there. The more we see of the unfolding of God's will, however, in the development of human society and in knowledge of the mechanics of the creation, the more it is clear that everything, and not just a selection of things, is in transition. The creation is progressive, not static; our understanding of the world is extremely imperfect, and our understanding of ultimate truths will not occur this side of death, yet we can engage the shifting values and culture of human society with reason and self-consciousness. Human sin gets injected into all our undertakings, including our attempts at understanding – but so it always has done, and it certainly did so in the primitive societies where the moral laws we have inherited took their first formal shape, and they are doubtless not untouched by the presence of sin in consequence.

The distinction between the *doctrines* and the *teachings* of the Church has always allowed Christian views about behaviour – matters of teaching – to be adjusted to circumstance. Doctrine conveys human perception of the nature of the divine, and is as unchanging as the divine nature is unchanging. Teaching concerns the moral relationships within human society, and necessarily changes according to adjustments within the social context. How many Christians, for example, now obey the dietary laws laid down very precisely in the Bible? The Bible also envisages a society in which the role of women was very different from the insights of contemporary culture, at any rate in the Western world. Christian men were once instructed by the Church on their duties as heads of families, but modern families are not supposed to have a paternalistic structure of internal authority, and the tax laws and divorce laws of modern states are adapting accordingly. The teachings of the Church in relation to human sexuality may also require adaptation.

Though doctrines are immutable, there is a theological tradition which contends that they may 'develop'. Doctrinal truths implicit in the community of the believers over centuries, that is to say, may be drawn out, under providence, to receive explicit recognition with the effluxion of time. Thus the Immaculate Conception, or the infallible office of the papacy, for Catholics. No doctrine may ever be dropped, however. Development is about bringing forth new things; but there must be no conflict with old doctrinal propositions.

Development as applied to *teachings* is rather different. Teaching is the application of doctrinal truth, as expressed in Christian living, to circumstance. Circumstances may alter so radically that new religious insights may actually replace preceding religious insights – as well as add to them. What meets the religious sense of one age may be inappropriate to the next, as the dialectic of faith and culture moves forward. The omission from new service books of the ancient service called 'The Churching of Women' in the Anglican Prayer Book is an instance. The old service seemed to suggest that after childbirth a woman needed to be purged of some impurity, as well as, more acceptably, providing thanksgiving for the birth. Centuries of teaching about sexual sin have been considerably modified in recent times, usually as a result of quiet adaptation by the clergy. Just a few years ago the Catholic priests in Ireland were directing their flocks about the moral evils of the dance hall; and everywhere the Church has given up regarding as sinful, all kinds of sexually provocative behaviour, provided it is heterosexual. Artificial means of birth control, condemned in high moral language at preceding Lambeth Conferences, was sanctioned at the Conference of 1930.

The threshold of offence changes with public acceptance. The tentative sexual experiments of teenage love, once condemned as fornication, are now seen as healthily acceptable. The best gauge of change is the response to sexually explicit references in film and television. These are no longer condemned by religious bodies (except the most sectarian), and it is violence rather than sexuality which today excites disapproval. Formal changes in Church teaching in relation to sexual custom are rare, and are mostly concerned with marriage discipline. This rarity is because the issues are always controversial, and the church leadership, anxious to proceed by consensus (or the appearance of it) prefers to arrange a series of pragmatic adaptations rather than countenance a full-blooded debate on matters of principle. The ecclesiastical authorities turn a blind eye to whatever the clergy want to teach on these matters, and uniformity of approach was long ago lost. Even the Catholic Church, with its centralized teaching office, and its structure of hierarchical authority, has in recent times allowed the local leadership to discuss adaptations of teachings in a limited but quite new fashion.

There are some aspects of human sexuality which have, in the past, always received the strictest condemnation within Christianity, and which are today still regarded by very many as outside the area of possible adaptation. Adultery, for example, or homosexuality, have never received anything but the clearest censure of ecclesiastical authority. But these kinds of issues ought not to be, as they inevitably are, lumped together as fixed parts of the moral code. They may be seen to be very different in nature when taken singly for consideration. Adultery, of the two instanced, involves deception and the violation of vows made before God; homosexual practices do not. Adultery is the fruit of human choice; homosexuals are born homosexuals, or are conditioned in sexual preference by circumstances of their earliest years over which they have no control – they are put together, that is to say, by God. Adultery places the children of marriage at risk; homosexuality may in some cases be experienced within a relationship which is permanent, but no other parties become immediately dependent on the survival of mutual faithfulness.

Plainly, in looking closely at the various expressions of human sexuality, in order to perform the prophetic task of determining what in Christian teaching is unchangeable and what may be adapted to altered circumstance, a very wide range of cultural as well as moral considerations will need to be canvassed. So must consciousness of human sin. Human relationships and sexual practices which appear to foster nothing but innocent gratification may in reality produce effects which are not easily calculable. Sin has a way of seeping into everything within the choice and capacity of men and women; and any who share the breezy contemporary assumption that people can control their own sexual impulses will learn the hard way that the wisdom of the ancients, rendered in sexual moral codes, sometimes had a core of unchangeable truth. But no one should be – as alas many are – put off Christianity because its teachings in this area are either too traditionalist or too liberal. The unstable balance between these poles has to be maintained if Christian truth is to advance in the only way it does: through the lives of men and women in the real world of their social exchanges.

18
Spiritual Nourishment

In view of the compulsive contemporary interest in the relationship, for bodily health, between what we eat and what we are, it is surprising that the same formula is not much applied to spiritual formation. Even within the churches there seems to be a little sense of urgency about instructing their own members in the need for planned spiritual nourishment, for the programming of spiritual enrichment by each individual. Now that society is so advanced in secularization, and the state is no longer charged with the maintenance of Christian values, the action of the Church in relation to its own members becomes of supreme importance: if men and women are to become spiritually educated they will need to envelop themselves in a spiritual culture. We are what we take in; if reading matter and the absorption of media information and entertainment is indiscriminate, the individual receives no structured formation in personal values. People always think they have the will and the intelligence to control their own spiritual well-being - they think they can prevent themselves being corrupted by corrupt literature, and that they do not need an explicit discipline to avoid interior moral chaos. But they are mistaken. What is needed, to put it bluntly, is self-censorship, and a framework of personal discipline which will allow the individual Christian believer to scrutinize and evaluate the nature of the data he or she absorbs.

It is sometimes said, by enlightened liberal parents, that they will allow their children to make their own decisions about religious belief, and that they will not prejudice the outcome with religious propaganda at an early age. What does that mean in practice? The values of society are going to be absorbed readily enough, and incorporated into the framework of the mind, through education and from the media. The moral imperatives of the contemporary secular culture are not going to be held delicately in reserve either: children are exposed from the earliest age to whatever issues at the time excite the moral seriousness of the secular intelligence. Since these are not usually associated with religion, except by the churches themselves (who have a great facility for claiming virtually any matter which preoccupies the moral concern of the intelligentsia as Christian) there is no automatic reason why children uninstructed in religious doctrine should feel the need for a religious dimension to their lives. If people are not brought up within spiritual references it is very much a matter of chance whether they will ever encounter any. In practice they may be moved by the example of Christian lives, or by the example of parents. But most attempts by individuals to lead Christian lives are not unambiguously successful, and it is their insufficiency, rather than their attainments, which is likely to strike the observer seeking personal inspiration.

The only effective means of providing spiritual nourishment is a balanced diet of spiritual food. This was well known to the religious leadership in traditional society, but is fearfully neglected by their successors in our own. How systematically do the clergy advise their flocks about what to read or which television programmes to watch, or about the choice of education? It would seem to many people an unacceptable interference with individual liberty if they did. In reality it is very much a matter of chance if any direction is received by Christians from their pastors about the mechanics of spiritual formation. Clergy feel intimidated by liberal distaste for prescribing propaganda; yet this is a world of propaganda, and if Christians do not supply their own nobody else will. The human community is given over to a compendium of ideologies: Christians are dangerously uninstructed in theirs.

There was never a time when there was a greater need for the churches to emphasize the importance of their traditional role in education. In many cases the educational institutions founded and conducted by the churches have become rather too much like their secular counterparts – sometimes, as church leaders of the last century predicted, it is the price to pay for accepting financial assistance from the state. There is no guarantee that the values promoted in the state schools will be compatible with religion in the future. Even at the present time they arguably encourage a degree of relativism over religious phenomena which promotes scepticism among children. Church schools, providing instruction in Christian doctrine, and associating the acquisition of secular knowledge with Christian values, are more crucial now than ever before if children are to receive spiritual formation. Few, alas, see it in this way.

The existing educational work of the Church is often, educationally, of the highest quality, especially in America, where

Catholic parochial schools have a distinguished record of providing a counter-culture to the secularism which the constitutional separation of Church and state has necessarily fostered in the public school system. In Britain the church authorities can point out that the financial resources available would not be adequate to sustain a network of educational institutions if they were not in receipt of large government subsidies, and that a diluted Christian presence is better than none at all. It has to be said, on the other hand, that the main reason that the church schools are not uniformly confessional in tone is not financial but ideological: their managers are insufficiently clear about the nature of Christian education itself. But the matter is extremely urgent. Now that society in general, through its customs and through government, makes little provision for the teaching of exact Christian truth, it is up to the family and the Church to do so.

Recent legislation in England which appeared to reinforce the teaching of Christianity in schools is not likely to issue in any greater actual provision of Christian teaching, since neither the resources available nor the teaching profession itself seem set to revert to systematic instruction in Christian beliefs. The new law, in that particular, represents a moment of controversy; it satisfied contending parties at a fraught stage of the legislative process, and is a compromise form of words which seems remote from the real possibility of changed attitudes in the schools themselves, and especially in the secondary schools, where possible revisions of practice would have their most significant consequence.

Without public social support, Christian doctrines have to be taught in the family or in the Church. That means precise action, and the large-scale provision of literature and visual aids. It means, in short, systematic propaganda directed at believers. We are what we take in. At present almost all of this is left to chance; the assimilation of Christian truth has been randomized by Christians themselves, who appear to assume that it is still possible to absorb Christianity from the surrounding cultural atmosphere, without any special provision. No one who becomes an enthusiast for a political doctrine would dream of leaving the acquisition of specialist knowledge about it to chance in this way.

The choice of work, too, is often prompted by secular considerations rather than a sense of religious vocation. How many select their life's work, their means of livelihood and the way of maintaining a family, with reference to spiritual values? How many actually ask themselves if a particular employment is more or less likely than another to assist spiritual formation? For many, of course, the choices are limited by circumstance – of social class, educational attainment, geographical location, and so forth. But religious considerations are for most people not obviously decisive in the necessary calculations. Yet a major part of an adult life is passed in the work-place. Religious belief has become so marginated that many are prepared to regard it like a leisure activity: something done outside working hours. For Christians, however, work should itself be an important determinant in spiritual formation, an opportunity of service to others and a means of discovering the mechanics of spirituality in oneself. In traditional society the individual often had no choice about employment, and children were reared to do whatever the family occupation had always been. In traditional society, however, structured provision was made for the acquisition and nourishment of religious values, and the circumstances of life were arranged around the events of the Christian calendar.

Spiritual formation, then, like so much else in modern society, has been made a matter of private decision. It is one of the great virtues of a liberal society that this is so, and that no public authority may enforce religious belief. But the churches have never really sensed the importance of the change that has occurred – or quite appreciated that if they, or Christian families, do not do something about spiritual instruction in a planned and systematic fashion Christian truth will become more and more imprecise. In the end, perhaps, it will become a vague moralism, comparable, indeed, to the humanist morality of the secular culture. Even now the ignorance of Christian doctrines, among Christians themselves, can sometimes be quite startling when it is encountered.

A knowledge of revealed truth cannot be left to chance. It is, by definition, truth which has been received in special ways, by divine dispensation, and it needs special ways to be assimilated. The acquisition of spiritual truth, that is to say, has to be associated with prayer, and with a disciplined life which is, furthermore, maintained at a high level of consciousness. This is not a very evident feature of contemporary Christianity, and it is one of the impediments to faith, for those outside the churches, that Christians often do not seem to take their own beliefs – which are declared to be of supreme value – sufficiently seriously to make them matters of daily study. People vary about the best means of achieving spiritual formation. Some value Bible study, some devotional exercises, some meditative reflection, some reading from Christian literature. We are what we take in: whatever the preferred approach, the spiritual nourishment needs a plan and a system, and it needs to be conveyed to children. Parents who really believe in their religion can scarcely allow their children to be uninstructed in it. The secular moral culture leaves children in no doubt about the moral evils of racism, for example, or of the need for a moral basis to economic organization. Why should Christian parents not instruct their children in the doctrinal details of revealed truth?

In England higher education is particularly neglected by the churches. In Europe and America the churches have established colleges and universities; in England the religious authorities are content to maintain a Christian presence through chaplaincies at institutions which are not under their control. They are in fact living on borrowed time. The ancient universities were Christian institutions; their secularization occurred, characteristically for England, in a series of stages and without anyone allowing ideological considerations to receive coherence. The result is that the Church today has no direct means of participation in the conduct or extension of intellectual life. The nearest it gets is the surviving Colleges of Education under Anglican or Catholic trustees, and in these, indeed, very serious efforts are made to combine liberal education with the maintenance of confessional truth. But they are not, for all their vocational excellence, institutions which are at the forefront of intellectual advance. That is not their purpose. What the churches need is the establishment of Christian institutions of higher education which associate the work of individual spiritual formation with the pursuit of knowledge.

19
Black Christianity

The most vital and expansive segment of Christianity in England lies outside the mainstream churches. Much of black Christian belief is expressed within classic sects: small autonomous churches of those who, sensing themselves to be at the social periphery, discover a compensating identity through membership of a company of elevated initiates. Those who are disadvantaged in the material circumstances of life discover in exclusive religious organization a structure which transcends the meanness of daily living. The classic religious sect, described by Max Weber and Ernst Troeltsch, and examined in relation to South African experience in the important works of Benkt Sundkler and in relation to America by Elmer T. Clarke, is thriving in the urban *anomie* of late twentieth-century Britain – as it is also in cities throughout the world where external or internal migration has produced situations of social disorientation.

The exclusivity of the sects outlives its utility as the migrants integrate with society in the second generation, but by then fresh arrivals, or new internal movements of people, have taken over the organizations and perpetuated their vitality. Sects are in a steady state of flowering and dying: where there is social mobility and social deprivation, and a surviving popular culture which is able to find in religious experience a satisfactory vehicle for the searing aspirations of the dispossessed, they will always have an appeal. In their secularized form sects become apocalyptic versions of political creeds, and social upheaval may then be among the evidences of their appeal.

The black Christian sects of contemporary England are conservative bodies, however, which seek only the spiritual exaltation of their members, and the warmth of a human companionship which seems unattainable in the encompassing society of the white population. Most of the sects are extremely respectable, stressing personal honesty and the ethic of hard work; they are also markedly traditionalist over family values and religious understanding itself. Their religious styles, though externally appearing to be characterized by spontaneity and freedom from formal constraints, are in fact successful attempts to resuscitate folk memories of an ordered past of social and religious certainty, before the disruption which brought the members to the urban anonymity of their lives. Social causes would doubtless prompt the appearance of religious sectarianism within the black population whatever other conditions prevail, and the persistence of the phenomenon in many parts of the world shows how the 'store-front churches', as they are known in America, cater for needs which are universal, among poor whites as well as among blacks.

For all that, however, there are many who are attracted to the sects because the white churches have seemed to them to be unwelcoming. In America, indeed, historical divisions of the last century, originating in attitudes to the slavery question, resulted in separate black denominations as well as in sects; this institutionalizing of Christianity along racial lines has at least so far been avoided in England. The emergence of the black Christian sects in England, however, has produced a kind of practical religious *apartheid.* There are, it is true, a number of middle class blacks who have found themselves at home in the white denominations, but the huge appeal of the sects indicates that separate development of black and white churches has become the normal pattern. That is why it must be included in any consideration of the impediments to Christianity in contemporary society. A momentary reflection will suggest that where different races are only able to worship together in specialized circumstances, there is something wrong with the social basis of Christianity in general.

If sectarianism is an unavoidable and universal consequence of social dislocation it is bound to occur when conditions are suitable, whatever the white churches are like in their relation to potential black members. But the problem is peculiarly compounded by the class orientation of the white churches. Throughout the whole of the Western world, and even in countries with high levels of popular religious affiliation, like Poland or America or Ireland, the churches, and especially the Protestant churches, are plainly stamped with the social class characteristics of the middle classes. It is these, rather than any overt racial antipathies, which black people first encounter. Many blacks are socially ambitious, for themselves and for their children, and a consciousness of social class heightens their recognition that the class characteristics of the leading white denominations, about which they are not in general able to be articulate, any more than white working class people are, seem alien to their existing conditions.

The white church leadership has for long been aware of its intellectual and cultural removal from working class society, but its consequent class guilt is itself a class indicator. The adoption of progressive political stances, attempts to fashion styles of religious worship with popular resonances, clumsy if well-intentioned essays in cross-class camaraderie, have all been tried with little evident impact. The clergy are still overwhelmingly recruited from the middle classes – how can it realistically be otherwise in a class society? – and those who do have genuine working class origins undergo a process of embourgeoisement during the course of their training, and emerge, at the end of it, unaware of the extent to which their new professional capabilities are in fact class characteristics. In their cultural interests, their moral concerns, their reading-matter, and their preoccupation with public issues, the clergy of all the mainstream churches are clearly adherents of middle class values.

Black citizens seeking upward class movement do not, however, find much in common with white middle class Christianity. And this, sadly, is despite the many earnest efforts made by some white congregations in mixed-race areas to welcome black numbers. The gounds of social ease do not exist. Integration of blacks into the white churches is more readily accomplished in areas which are largely populated by whites: the relatively few blacks who can afford to live in the middle class suburbs have usually, already, undergone enough class adaptation to feel themselves sufficiently at home. In many places the white churches are so poorly attended that new members, black or white, find there is little to join anyway – and certainly nothing which is going to assist a general social integration. It is less painful and less socially embarrassing to join a crowd than it is a handful of people – unless the handful is already of what you consider your own sort. Hence the appeal of the sect. Successful white churches tend to be the result not of conversions or of the gathering of lost members: they are the consequence of cannibalizing the churches of the surrounding catchment area; their expansion, usually due to the energy of a particular clergyman, is at the expense of other churches.

Black Christians have no need of all this. Why should they

bother to worship with the whites, with all the differences of social class that have to be accommodated in order to do so, when they can organize worship for themselves? There is a problem of religious custom, too. Black worship is more formal than it looks, in the sense that the spontaneity of the worshippers is actually quite stylized and occurs within recognized conventions. There is wide variation. Not all black churches are Pentecostal or charismatic, though most of the sects in some sense are. Despite apparent similarities, the charismatic exercises found within some of the white churches, of all denominations, do not provide a bridge between the races. The emotional release of the black churches and sects is somehow more authentic, in that it has immediate echoes of a living folk culture, and is a natural part of a total set of human responses. Older blacks can still remember the fulness of that culture as lived in the country of origin, before the trauma of emigration. Emotional informality in white churches is much more a matter of symbolism. Because white culture does not encourage public displays of emotion, worship which is emotionally demonstrative is necessarily episodic: it is unlike normal life. Some, doubtless, experience what in other circumstances would be recognized as involuntary hysterical spasms and other manifestations of momentary psychic disorientation or cultural catharsis. Most, however, are conscious beneficiaries of staged informality. The two groups of styles found in black and in white churches do encounter some overlap, but that is not a very common experience.

This all makes for sombre reflection. Many will of course say that in *their* church it is all quite different, and that black members feel comfortably at home. It is precisely because white Christians are so unperceptive about the real feelings of black people that the matter needs to be raised in its starkest form. Most black Christianity is not only attractively vital in itself, it is also orthodox in doctrine, biblical, and expansive. It is, like the Christianity of the non-European world – which in many places (in Africa and Asia) is stimulated by contact with the contemporary dynamism of Islam – a living force in the life of its members. To what extent can that be said to be true of white adherents of Christianity? Here all the questioning and the loss of confidence which characterizes a dying culture are to be found; here are a wide range of substitutes for religion, and a pervasive sense that moral engagement with the great issues of material survival or social justice are more important than personal attachment to a religious creed. Black Christianity has been neither privatized nor individualized. It is something that involves the whole life of the believer; it is also a group experience, rather than something that is fashioned in response to the intellectual fastidiousness of the individual. There is always some risk of romanticizing the black sects: there are many different patterns, and not all fit this profile. Some are too exclusivist. But the primary concern of most black Christianity is the spiritual formation of the believers. And that is where white Christians have much to rediscover.

20
Authentic Religion

The secularized Western mind now finds it difficult to regard Christianity as a *religion.* It can accommodate Christian ethics readily enough, and it recognizes the emotional utility to individuals of a belief-structure which has therapeutic effects. Christianity has historical roots which assist the interpretation of received culture; it fosters social order and generally encourages human decency. Even among the most convinced Christian believers themselves, whose minds are often no less secularized through immersion in the prevailing secular culture, there is sometimes little sense that religion involves the whole of experience. Western pilgrims to the Holy Land, for example, are often appalled by the evidences of authentic religion which they encounter. The over-familiarity of adherents with the most sacred of their own rites, the arcane ritual practices, the 'fanaticism' of those who carry religious convictions into daily life, even the absence of sanitized places of worship: these seem to Westerners to be indications, not of the patina of faith, but of ignorance.

But Christianity is a religion. It shows the characteristics of all religions. The divine is disclosed to humanity through the natural order and through revelation. In the natural order the existence of God is indicated through observation of the relationship between men and their environment, both the physical and the cultural environment. In revealed truth - in Christianity - God confirms the insights of the natural order and additionally offers the gifts of forgiveness and salvation. But the nature of the religion of the natural order is not, in the process, destroyed, and a religious confession which fails to recognize its continuity with its own origins will be insensitive in its relations with religious professions which are untouched by revealed truth, and will itself become spiritually desiccated. The first sign of this, as the history of Christianity has shown, is that religious experience becomes progressively confined to cerebral activity - people worship with a book in their hands, and only respect religion when it is all about cosmic explanation. The second sign is that religion is regarded as most mature when it has become essentially an ethical system.

Authentic religion evokes the reality of the unseen world; it is a means of touching mystery and of sensing the exterior boundaries of unknowable truths. It facilitates communion with the dead, for it comprises a realm where the barriers between life and eternal life are diaphanous, and in which the divine power is not divided into the spatial spheres which men and women inhabit. Religion is a matter of initiation: its truths are not immediately apparent, but require instruction into doctrines and the traditions of religious transmission inherited from the past. There are rites in which the new adherent is ritually cleansed. Religion is about the acknowledgement of the celestial forces, whose sovereignty over the world can be ignored only at the greatest peril: for God is judgement. Religion involves fear of God, whose rule is absolute, and demands the complete allegiance of those to whom he has given consciousness and life. It is, above all, mystery.

Traditional religion pointed out the evidences of the divine presence in the natural state of the world, and it showed, also, how divinity indicated its will to mankind. There were myths of creation and of the final destruction, and the rotation of the seasons and the fertility of living things were related to the benevolent intentions of God. What traditional religion did not provide, however, was an explanation of the *meaning* of human life itself, or of the detailed sensations of men. These things were the direct prerogative of God; they were all divine mystery. Modern humanity, of course, has successfully asked all kinds of questions about the mechanics of the creation, and it has sometimes been possible to show how some of these answers account for human phenomena which had been traditionally ascribed to divine mystery. Of the rest humanity is impatient for explanation, and regards religious belief as only intellectually tenable if it begins to furnish, not mystery, but keys for unlocking the heavenly treasury. In its contemporary understanding of religion the Western mind finds little room for what is actually its very substance: divine mystery.

Religion is also about the corruption of the world. This is something far more extensive than the total of the corruption of individual men and women. In the traditional religious vision the world itself was seen to be out of joint, and the highest aspirations of humanity, its most noble essays in altruism, were realized to be flawed and ambiguous. The seeds of corruption were in all things, and the earth was enveloped in a constant state of evil, to which men and women approximated in varying degrees of consciousness. Religious assistance could alleviate the consequences of human frailty, and religion might be able to provide ultimate redemption if adherents attended to their duties. Yet the pervasive sin of the world was a dead-weight which special grace alone could overcome. In the pagan religions it could be overcome through the special favour of the gods.

The Christian doctrine that salvation is a free gift of God, which men cannot earn through their own enterprise, should be evaluated against this pagan acceptance of the notion that humans could make bargains with the gods about their ultimate fate. The Jewish concept of the Covenant had pagan echoes – it was actually expressed in formularies which simulated the treaties made between contracting parties in the world. The Christian New Covenant was thus radical in departing from an important dimension of traditional religion. But it was still a Covenant, one which was sealed by the sacrifice of God himself, and which gave men, not explanation and meaning, but salvation. Religious continuity is important for an appreciation of Christianity. The Old Testament and the New are equal in value, though different in purpose: the one describes the historical action of God as he revealed himself to his people, and the other reveals the dynamics of redemption. Christians sometimes regard the New Testament as having replaced the Old, but that is to decline a progressive view of revelation, and thus to devalue the Scriptures which Christ himself knew. 'Isn't it wonderful the appeal of the Bible', said the beetle to the grass in Joe Orton's *Head to Toe*; 'I prefer the New Testament to the Old myself, though I suppose there is less to interest a plant.'

A sense of impermanence, of the transience of human values and associations, is also a characteristic of traditional religion. This is sometimes combined with a stark apocalyptic vision, in which the order of the world is overthrown and the kingdom of the saints is inaugurated. The days are seen to be evil, and there is urgency about the need for sins to be confessed and expiated. Apocalyptic drama plainly existed in the message of Christ, who called his followers from the evils of the world into the austerities of deserted places, and preached an impending Kingdom in which the poor would be exalted, the rich cast down, and the first become the last. But the idea of inherent corruption does not significantly appeal to those who, like the men and women of today, have a heightened regard for the virtues of humanity, and whose doctrine of human rights enshrines entitlements not judgements. Contemporary society does not relish the apocalyptic vision, except in a secularized form – as in the thrilled expectation of ecological catastrophe or the possibility of nuclear incineration. It values social stability, and seeks a world of security in which even the most trivial hazards are subject to human control.

It is hardly surprising, in these circumstances, that the status of Christianity as a *religion* has been in some measure diminished by its own adherents. And in some things that was the correct thing to have done. For the message of Christ was a new dispensation; the world's history was divided forever when the Son of Man wept over the Holy City and died for the sins of ordinary men and women. Humanity is called to participate in the unfolding of the divine creative purpose – though necessarily, as created beings, still in ignorance of the grand design of life. Called to the dignity of joint-labour, however, men went beyond their vocation, and reached out to grasp the heavens themselves. Now they reject a religious scheme which never, anyway, promised meaning: only the discovery of the splendours of the creation. God invited them to probe the workings of things, so that they might advance the values he had given them, by employing the laws of creation for further creative achievements. He did not tell them the secret of creation itself – what things work *for*. It is the ultimate paradox: meaning is given to human life (and texture, and substance, and value) by the apparent meaninglessness of life itself. Men and women are called to a journey, a pilgrimage. The destination is beyond the horizon; the architecture of the heavenly city cannot be discerned from the only available perspectives.

Christianity is therefore to be seen as by nature a religion, similar in kind to the other religious phenomena of successive human experience. It is a religion which is, nonetheless, special because it transcends preceding religious dimensions. The religion of ancient society encouraged fatalistic acceptance in the world, and the place of individuals within it; Christianity stimulates creative engagement with the world, and offers personal knowledge of the creator. Yet it is, for all that, earthly, and its adherents are conditioned by the corruption which envelops human life and which, demonstrably enough, brings mocking chaos to the aspirations of those who expect human autonomy to accompany the work of creative discovery.

A religion which sheds its cultic characteristics, which dispels the sense of mystery in order to seek truth in the categories of rationality, which develops its ethical system without a corresponding emphasis upon its spiritual disciplines, which becomes preoccupied with the material fate of mankind and neglects its unique understanding of human transcendence, and which regards itself as most cogently expressed in movements for social advance, will cease to relate to the spiritual needs of humanity. The interior life of man is not social. Wisdom recognizes the loneliness of the creature in the cold realities of the creation, and it sees that what most afflicts the human soul is not susceptible to merely human consolation. The desolation of men and women is actually their natural state: the family, society, the nation, cultural forms and institutional identities, are all buffers against the terrifying truth that they are moving in a dimension of darkness. Is the illumination of religious faith just another of the buffers to reality? Many have thought so.

The light of Christian truth is not powerfully evident, either, for it is carried as a torch in the hands of men – the succession of believers to whom the Saviour first entrusted it. That the whole created order is actually suffused with light is not apparent to those whose angle of perspective is disjointed by sin. Christians believe that the larger radiancy, directed by the Holy Spirit, is the final vision of those who persist to the end. The darkness of the interim, however, crowds in upon the individual soul, and those whose spiritual instincts have not been entirely diverted by the preoccupations of life will recognize at once that it is human loneliness which is the source of religious understanding. The inventive capacity of the godless world, and all its confidence about the needs of men, is nowhere less appealing than in the loneliness of soul. The comedy of human life can only really be appreciated by those who no longer have a stake in its material outcome.